Baseball
in the Carolinas

ALSO BY CHRIS HOLADAY

Professional Baseball in North Carolina:
An Illustrated City-by-City History, 1901–1996
(McFarland, 1998)

BY CHRIS HOLADAY AND MARSHALL ADESMAN

The 25 Greatest Baseball Teams
of the 20th Century Ranked
(McFarland, 2000)

Baseball in the Carolinas

25 Essays on the States' Hardball Heritage

Edited by CHRIS HOLADAY

with a foreword by CLYDE KING

McFarland & Company, Inc., Publishers
Jefferson, North Carolina, and London

All royalties from the sale of this book will be donated to the North Carolina Baseball Museum in Wilson, North Carolina.

Library of Congress Cataloguing-in-Publication Data

Baseball in the Carolinas : 25 essays on the states' hardball
 heritage / edited by Chris Holaday with a foreword by Clyde
 King.
        p.   cm.
     Includes index.

     ISBN-13: 978-0-7864-1318-8
     (softcover : 50# alkaline paper) ∞

     1. Baseball—North Carolina—History.   2. Baseball—
 South Carolina—History.   I. Holaday, J. Chris, 1966–

     GV863 .B33 2002
     796.357'09756—dc21
                                        2002001438

British Library cataloguing data are available

On the cover: High Point–Thomasville Hi-Toms manager Jimmy
Brown discusses strategy with pitcher Rene Solis and outfielder
Danny Morejon in 1955 *(courtesy of High Point Museum archives).*

Manufactured in the United States of America

*McFarland & Company, Inc., Publishers
  Box 611, Jefferson, North Carolina 28640
   www.mcfarlandpub.com*

To every Carolinian who has ever picked up
a bat and ball or slipped a glove on his hand.
To the coaches, the umpires, and those who have
filled the stands cheering for their favorite team.
You are all part of what makes the great game
of baseball in the Carolinas what it is today.

Best Wishes
to Brandom,
Alex Cosmidis

Acknowledgments

I would like to thank everyone who has helped to make this project a reality, particularly the contributing authors. They were all so willing to share their knowledge and expertise.

I would also like to thank Ann Wright at Pack Memorial Library in Asheville, Linda McCormick at North Carolina State University Library, and Larry Tarleton and Pam Liles at the *Charleston Post and Courier*. Dylan Jenkins was also a big help on the technical side of things.

Gratitude goes as well to two prominent baseball historians: John Pardon, for compiling the stats on Manley Llewellyn and Bobby Hipps, and Jim Sargent, for his AAGPBL photos.

I am honored that a baseball figure as prominent as Clyde King would write a foreword for this book. A native North Carolinian, Clyde has done it all in baseball. His professional résumé, which covers nearly 60 years, includes such jobs as pitcher for the Brooklyn Dodgers and the Cincinnati Reds, and manager of three big league clubs: the San Francisco Giants, the Atlanta Braves, and the New York Yankees. Currently he is employed by the Yankees as a special assistant.

Though he didn't directly contribute to this book I would also like to acknowledge Lee Gliarmis of Wilson, North Carolina. A truly great "baseball man," his dedication to the game and preserving its heritage inspired me.

Most of all, thanks to my wife Sue for putting up with me while I was working on this project.

I would also like to mention that Hank Utley's stories in this book are based on figures in *The Independent Carolina Baseball League,*

1936–1938 (McFarland, 1999), the book he co-authored with Scott Verner. For those interested in learning more, Hank has donated his entire collection of research and photographs to the Robinson-Spangler Carolina Room at the Charlotte Public Library.

Contents

Foreword

by Clyde King

The book *Baseball in the Carolinas* is a classic! It takes readers back to the early years of baseball in North and South Carolina and brings them up to the present day. From personal experience, having written a book myself, *A King's Legacy*, I can appreciate the time, effort, and extensive research that all of the contributors have put into this outstanding history of our national pastime in the Carolinas.

Baseball has been a great part of my life and a huge influence on me since the age of eight. I played neighborhood baseball, high school baseball, American Legion baseball, semi-pro baseball, college baseball and finally Major League baseball for many years. Baseball kept me on the diamond and off the street corners, out of poolrooms and other places I should not have been. And, in fact, it kept me out of trouble. *Baseball in the Carolinas* will not only bring back wonderful memories, but it will cause us to realize what a fantastic role these two states have

One of North Carolina's most accomplished "baseball men," Goldsboro native Clyde King made his pitching debut with the Brooklyn Dodgers at the age of 20 and went on to spend seven seasons in the big leagues. A great student of the game, King turned to a managerial role when he gave up the mound and eventually spent time at the helm of the San Francisco Giants, the Atlanta Braves and the New York Yankees. He currently serves as a special assistant to Yankees owner George Steinbrenner.

played—and continue to play—in promoting this great game. At one time North Carolina had more professional teams and more players in the major leagues than any other state. South Carolina has a rich history in the game and has produced its fair share of talented ballplayers as well.

I remember when I was ten years old I would go out to old Griffin Park in Goldsboro with my brothers Claude (who also played professional baseball) and Billy to watch our hometown team, the Goldbugs, play. We didn't have any money to buy tickets, so we waited outside the park behind the home plate area for a foul ball that would come over the little grandstand during practice. When a ball came over the fence all of us (maybe ten kids or more) would fight for it with all our strength. When my brothers and I each got a ball we would give them back to the club and they would let us in for free. That's how much we loved baseball at that young age.

Two of my favorite players for the Goldbugs were left fielder Sam Patton and first baseman Eddie Ignasiak. My favorite pitchers were Terry Pollock, Bill Herring, Julio Acosta (who had a great move to first base) and Don Kepler (who I tailored my windup from). These players never went on to become big league stars, but to us kids they were our heroes. I still remember their names 60 years later—that's how important they were to us. This was where and when baseball really got in my blood. It has been there ever since. The 2001 season was my 57th in pro ball. Baseball has been good to me!

I remember another story about an important game from my youth. When I was 15 years old I was playing on a men's team for the Borden Mills Co. in Goldsboro. It was a Saturday afternoon game in Selma, N.C., and I was the pitcher. I hit my first home run over the fence in that game; I had hit a couple before but not over the fence. The ball went in the cornfield behind right field, and before the outfielder could find it I rounded the bases! We were leading 2 to 1 in the bottom of the ninth inning, with no one on base and two outs. Up came a former minor league player named Harvey Pittman. Now Harvey had been a real good hitter in the lower minor leagues. I was told he hit .400 one year. The umpire in those days stood behind the pitcher to call balls and strikes. Harvey hit a high fly ball down the left field line and the umpire went over to third base to see if it would be foul or fair. Suddenly, I heard footsteps and turned around just in time to see Pittman coming right over the pitcher's mound on his way to second base. He almost ran over me! This means, of course, that he did not go to first base but left the batter's box and headed straight to second via the mound. We were all yelling at the ump that he did not touch first base and the ump said, "I can't call him out because I didn't see him do that." Now that was great thinking that only a veteran ball player would think of. This taught me a lesson: use your head but stay within the rules. Harvey didn't do that! I was fortunate to get the next batter out and we won, but Mr. Pittman almost stole the game!

The names of the cities, towns, and crossroads mentioned in *Baseball in the Carolinas* really bring back many wonderful memories for me, names out of the past I had forgotten. It also makes me remember just how important the game has always been in the two states. So, to those of you who read this book and have old memories stirred up, and to those of you who discover this history for the first time, it will be interesting and informative. I hope you will enjoy it as much as I did.

Introduction

by Chris Holaday

It is unknown when the game of baseball first made its way from the North down to the Carolinas. It was being played in the two states at least as early as the Civil War; a famous lithograph from 1862 shows Union soldiers in the Confederate prison camp at Salisbury, N.C., celebrating the Fourth of July with a baseball game. By the early years of the 20th century, baseball had become *the* form of entertainment across the Carolinas. On many evenings and Saturday afternoons, entire populations of small towns would turn out to watch their local nine take on a team from a neighboring town.

The textile industry was among the biggest supporters of the game up until the 1950s. Early on, mill owners discovered that baseball was a great way to boost morale and promote a sense of community. Rivalries between mills became intense and some reached legendary status. It was not uncommon for mill owners to put professional ball players on the payroll just for the purpose of having them play baseball.

The game at the professional level has always been well represented in the Carolinas, first appearing in 1886 when the Charleston Seagulls joined the Southern League. In the first decade of the 20th century, minor league baseball clubs began to spring up in other cities, including Charlotte, Greensboro, and Columbia. That growth continued, and during the heyday of minor league ball, the years right after World War II, more than 50 different towns and cities in the two states had professional teams to call their own.

In the early 1950s, the game in the Carolinas changed as people began to discover new sources of entertainment, particularly television. Minor league baseball died out in all but a handful of cities. It wasn't until the early 1980s that Carolinians rediscovered their love of small-town professional baseball. Teams began to reappear, old stadiums were refurbished and new state-of-the-art parks were built. In 2001, ten minor league teams played in North Carolina while four more made their homes in South Carolina.

The Carolinas have also been the home to many great collegiate baseball programs. Clemson University, which has made it to the College World Series seven times, is one of the college game's legendary programs. Not far behind are both the University of North Carolina and the University of South Carolina. Both have made it to the College World Series several times, and South Carolina finished as national runners-up in 1975 and 1977. Despite the successes of these schools, none of them have ever won a national title. The only Division I school in the two states to claim that honor is Wake Forest University, who were national runners-up in 1949 and champions in 1955. Even some of the smaller schools in the Carolinas have fared well in intercollegiate play: North Carolina Wesleyan took Division III national titles in 1989 and 1999. East Carolina University, now a perennial Division I baseball power, won the NAIA national title in 1961, while High Point (1979) and Winthrop (1981) have been NAIA runners-up.

During the summer, many top college players sharpen their skills and prepare themselves for a possible career in professional baseball by participating in the Coastal Plain League. Nine of the eleven teams that make up this premier wooden-bat league are located in the two states. The college stars of tomorrow can be found playing in one of the countless great high school programs in the region or spending their summers playing American Legion ball. The Carolinas have produced five National Champions of this highly competitive organization (Gastonia 1935, Spartanburg 1936, Albemarle 1940, Shelby 1945, Charlotte 1965) as well as six second place finishers (Columbia 1931, Spartanburg 1938, Albemarle 1944, Gastonia 1954, Charlotte 1964, Cherryville 1998).

The Carolinas have seen their fair share of major league baseball as well. It was once common for big league teams to stage exhibition games in various cities while traveling home to the North after spring training in Florida. The two states have actually been the site of spring training for many clubs, particularly those in the minor leagues. While a member of the then–minor league Baltimore Orioles, the mighty Babe Ruth reportedly hit his first home run as a professional during spring training in Fayetteville.

Seven players from North Carolina (Hoyt Wilhelm, Buck Leonard, Gaylord Perry, Enos Slaughter, Jim "Catfish" Hunter, Luke Appling, and Rick Ferrell) have gone on to achieve the game's highest honor: enshrinement in the Baseball Hall of Fame in Cooperstown, N.Y. South Carolina can boast one Hall of Famer (Larry Doby) and another (Joe Jackson) who certainly has the credentials to be a member.

No matter what the level of the game, residents of the Carolinas have a love of baseball. From the five-year-old kids just learning tee-ball to the professional athletes playing just one level below the major leagues, the game is played by thousands of great and not-so-great athletes in the two states. Some play it hoping for a career in the sport, but most play it just because they love the game. Though the monopoly it once enjoyed for the attentions of fans is long gone and other sports have grown in popularity, baseball will always hold a special place in the hearts and lives of Carolinians. Hopefully this book captures some of that passion.

Greensboro, 1954

by Miles Wolff

It is approaching fifty years. Can it be such a long time ago, when the memories from that year are stronger, clearer than most from recent years? I discovered baseball in 1954, and for a ten year old I was discovering something that would change my life. We had moved to a new neighborhood in Greensboro, and I didn't know any of the guys in the neighborhood yet. The ballpark was a mile and a half from our house, and when my Sunday school teacher (a stockholder in the club) gave me some tickets, I started going to the games. My parents would let me go by myself, and I felt grown up being able to go and be part of this largely adult, male crowd without my parents nearby.

The names were special, and I can remember almost every one. My heroes had names like Syl McNinch, John Patula, Eddie Irons and Hal Toso. The infield with Jake Charvat and Johnny Pfeiffer was terrific and set a Carolina League record for double plays. Center fielder Dick McCarthy was my special hero because he taught me how to catch a fly ball at a Little League clinic. And the best was catcher Guy Morton who

---

Miles Wolff did pursue a career in professional baseball, and at one time or another over the past thirty years has owned or run clubs in Savannah (GA), Asheville (NC), Pulaski (VA), Utica (NY), Jacksonville (FL), Anderson (SC) and Butte (MT). He is currently the president of Burlington in the Appalachian League and Quebec City in the Northern League.

Greensboro Patriots, 1954

This picture courtesy of *Pilot Life Insurance Company*, sponsors of *Patriot* ball games, broadcast by *Add Penfield* over *WBIG*.

led the league in hitting and had 32 home runs. I was certain all were destined for major league stardom, but only one made it, Morton, who was called up at the end of the season by the Red Sox. He became our own "Moonlight" Graham as he made one major league appearance as a pinch hitter. He struck out.

There was something magic in walking through those huge concrete arches into a building with sights and sounds and smells I had never, ever experienced. Not that it was grand when compared with modern stadia, but for me it was terribly special. The passageways under the grandstand were narrow and dark and a little scary, but if you turned to the right and went about fifty feet, you might run into a player coming out of the clubhouse walking through the fans to the dugout. Turn to the left and you would find the rest rooms, dirty and smelly and painted in an off shade of brown that did nothing to make them more attractive. But it was fun to take a pee in that long trough. The concessions were small and cramped but no one went to baseball games to eat. The seats were wood with splinters, and the front walkway between the field and the stands had yet to be paved, but for me it was the most marvelous place I could imagine.

War Memorial Stadium in the fifties was showing the same deterioration of baseball facilities as many stadiums across the country as interest in the minors declined. The stadium was used for practically every baseball event in the city—the Carolina League games, American Legion, semi-pro and the Negro league games. In the fall, A&T College football was played there, along with junior high football. Even my 8th grade midget league football games were played on the scraggly grass. At an earlier time a cinder running track had circled through the outfield, and the outline of the track and many of the cinders remained in right field. When it was completed in 1926, it was an 8,000-seat memorial to those who died in the Great War, one of the largest multi-purpose stadiums in the state. Initial plans were to increase the capacity to 20,000, but it never came to be, and because of its location in a decaying, older neighborhood, the stadium became an afterthought in the life of a growing city.

The rhythms of baseball quickly became the rhythms of my life. There was spring training with its anticipation. Opening Day was hope. The first month was full of expectations, then mid-season became reality, and August moved on to endurance. Finally fall brought relief, and with winter quiet and only an occasional mention of baseball in the newspaper. The rhythms of radio play-by-play washed over me, and at night under

Opposite: The 1954 Greensboro Patriots. (Photograph courtesy of Chris Holaday.)

the covers I would listen to Add Penfield on WBIG as he taught me the language and clichés of baseball.

We lived in an older section of Greensboro, and with our neighborhood close to the stadium, people rented rooms for the summer to players. Jimmy McGee lived up the street, and he found out that two of the Patriots were living in the big house on the corner over the orthodontist's office. With that fearlessness that makes being a kid special we rushed over to the house, ran up the stairs and knocked on the door, certain the players would be overjoyed to see two scruffy kids asking for an autograph. We had no concept that players went to bed late and got up late, and a sleepy young man answered the door, signed our slips of paper and said maybe later in the day he might come out and talk with us. Hugh Murray lived over on Cyprus Street with his grandmother. She rented rooms to players. We were amazed to see one of the outfielders, Freddie Duval, sitting on her front porch reading the Bible. We knew ball players did a lot of things, but reading the Bible was new.

I learned so much from baseball, some important things and also those pieces of trivia that baseball fans regurgitate at any opportunity. I learned math and how to keep averages. I learned geography as I looked on maps to see where Greensboro players were born or where they were being sent, to San Jose or Bluefield or Allentown. I learned how to read a newspaper and box scores, and the sports section led to the front pages and real news. I learned to boo the umpires and keep score. I learned how to play hitters so I could get foul balls, and I learned the value of money and how to spend correctly.

My mother would give me three dimes before I left for the park, and at the second, fourth and sixth innings I would walk down to the sno-cone stand and order a cherry or grape or lime sno-cone. Lime was the best. The sno-cones were only a dime (the hot dogs twenty cents), and there was certainly none of the high cuisine that has infected the modern minor league park. Everything was basic about Memorial Stadium. These shaved pieces of ice with colored water were all I ever ordered at the park, but I loved them, and when the ice was fresh, and an extra squirt of juice was given by the man behind the counter, life couldn't get much better.

I also learned some things that were not so special. I learned about race. Greensboro worked with the Yankees and the Red Sox, and there were no black ball players on our teams for many years. Burlington and Danville were breaking the color barrier in the league, but Greensboro fans held a perverse sense of superiority in having a lily-white team. The foulest names and taunts were reserved for those players that happened to have a darker skin. One little section at the end of the first base grandstand was reserved for the black fans, with its own small rest rooms underneath, but that was all that was needed, for only a handful of black fans ever patronized the team. Even on the impressive bronze plaques on the front entrance to the stadium, where those killed during the First World War were listed, the names were segregated, with a separate column for the colored dead. One black vendor roamed the stands with soft drinks. A few of the good ol' boys who populated the third base lines would yell out "Snowball," and when he brought them cokes, other racial names were used. He always had this fixed smile on his face and I wondered how he could keep his good nature. A few years later, when the sit-in demonstrations started in downtown Greensboro, I remember seeing him marching. I understood.

For the next five or six years my summers were spent going to the games, probably fifty or sixty a year. And the crowds kept getting smaller and I couldn't understand why. I loved the games, but usually there were only five or six hundred die-hards cheering the Patriots and later the G-Yanks. The team started promoting, and there were Pony Nights and Tropical Pet Night, and acts like Jackie Price and Max Patkin, and for a game or two there might be a spurt in attendance but then it would fall off. Some nights the team would give out free tickets, but the people at those games never came back. Each fall there were rumors that the team would leave. By the time I was fifteen or sixteen, with the arrogance of youth, I knew I could do a better job, that I could make people come to the games and enjoy them as much as I did. And I knew what I wanted to do with the rest of my life. Baseball had grabbed me and has never let go.

Talent for the Game

by Chris Holaday

Though his involvement with professional baseball has spanned more than 40 years, the name Alex Cosmidis is probably not as familiar to baseball fans as it should be. Once a slick-fielding infielder, Cosmidis spent eleven seasons as a minor league player, another eight as a minor league manager and since 1982 has been a big league scout.

After graduating from high school in Norfolk, Virginia, in 1946, Alex Cosmidis went on to play baseball for Illinois Wesleyan University. He spent his summers playing for a semi-pro team in the town of Colerain, North Carolina, and in 1950 Cosmidis attracted the eye of the Chicago White Sox. They signed him and sent him to their Class C farm club in Hot Springs, Arkansas, where he finished the season as Cotton States League co–MVP.

Cosmidis spent the entire decade of the 1950s working his way up the minor league ladder, with stops in towns that included Waterloo, IA, Gastonia, NC, and Nashville, TN. He spent three seasons with Dallas and, while there, set a Texas League record of 66 errorless games at second

---

The highlight of Chris Holaday's brief baseball career came at age 15 when, as a high school freshman, he was selected to pitch in the varsity's annual marathon fundraising game. Being a first baseman he thought this unusual but didn't complain. It turned out that "pitcher" actually meant being the guy who fed balls into the pitching machine.

base. In 1957 he won the Rawlings Silver Glove Award for the best minor league fielder at his position. Cosmidis eventually spent two seasons at the AAA level, including stints with Portland in the Pacific Coast League and Rochester in the International League, but never received the call to take that final step to the big leagues. "I played with some good ones," Cosmidis says, "especially at Dallas. We had Willie McCovey, Jim Davenport, and Joe Amalfitano. I'd have to say Bill White was the best, though. He could do so many things for you. He was quick, he could steal a base and could hit for power."

With his playing career ended by a knee injury in 1960, Cosmidis decided to pursue a career as a manager. In 1961 he guided Salisbury, NC, one of the first two farm clubs for the expansion Houston franchise, to a Western Carolina League pennant. He still has a congratulatory telegram from Houston farm director Tal Smith for bringing the organization its first pennant. Cosmidis' managerial career then took him to Salem, VA, Appleton, WI, and Asheville, NC, among others. His final job as manager before leaving baseball for a new career in real estate came with Kinston, NC, of the Carolina League, in 1970. When asked who were some of the best players he had managed, Cosmidis thought for a moment. "I guess I would say Dave Concepcion and Kurt Bevacqua [Asheville in '69], Dave May [Salem in '62], Tito Fuentes [Salem in '63] and Carlos May [Appleton in '67 and Lynchburg in '68]."

Cosmidis finally returned to baseball in 1982 when he took a job as an area scout with the California Angels. Since 1987 he has worked for the Chicago White Sox, covering a three state area made up of North Carolina, South Carolina, and Virginia. Cosmidis' scouting has produced some talented players; his signees include former Angels star reliever Bryan Harvey, Kansas City Royals relief pitcher Roberto Hernandez (drafted out of the University of South Carolina–Aiken), Seattle Mariners pitcher James Baldwin and current White Sox infielder Ray Durham. Baldwin was found at Pinecrest High School in Southern Pines, NC, while Durham was discovered at Charlotte's Harding High School.

Two of his more recent finds are highly regarded pitching prospects Curtis Whitley and Pat Daneker, who were both drafted in 1997. Daneker, a fifth-round pick out of the University of Virginia, got called up to Chicago for "a cup of coffee" at the end of the 1999 season. He spent the 2000 season with Charlotte in the AAA International League before being traded to the Toronto Blue Jays. Whitley, discovered at North Carolina's Mount Olive College, was with AA Birmingham in 2000 and has had setbacks due to injury but is steadily working his way up in the White Sox organization. In the 2000 baseball draft Cosmidis was responsible for the selection of Old Dominion University shortstop Tim Hummel. A talented hitter and fielder, Hummel played well as a rookie in the Midwestern League and was promoted to Winston-Salem near the end of the season, where he continued to perform.

Though he is at an age where most people are enjoying their retirement, Cosmidis has no plans for saying goodbye to the game he loves. "I guess I'll keep doing this as long as I can," he says. "I've never been one to be much of a couch potato." Obviously not, as he travels 25–35,000 miles and attends close to 120 games every baseball season all across the three state area.

Somewhere out there is the next big league star. Maybe he is playing at a major university or maybe at a small town high school, but if he is in the Carolinas or Virginia, chances are Alex Cosmidis will find him.

Last Bus to Durham

by David Beal

There are a lot of "mysteries" that still surround the life of a minor league baseball player. Most of them have been solved by the vast array of media attention that has covered the minors in recent years. But one—the bus trip—still has a story to tell that only the true baseball fan can fully appreciate.

This is an account of August 30, 1997. On that Saturday, the Winston-Salem Warthogs made their last bus trip to Durham to play the Bulls. In 1998 a new Durham franchise (still called the Bulls) would join the ranks of Triple A ball and become an affiliate of the Tampa Bay Devil Rays. The Carolina League Bulls would be renamed and relocated—first to Danville, Virginia, for one season and then on to a permanent home in Myrtle Beach, South Carolina. This trip was history in the making and would not disappoint anyone who traveled that day.

I have been lucky to work as a front office volunteer for more than a decade in Winston-Salem. A lot has happened at Ernie Shore Field during that time, but some of my favorite memories have been on road trips with the team. This last one to Durham was special, and thanks to Manager Mark Haley and General Manager Pete Fisch, I got clearance to

David Beal of Mount Airy, NC, led a semi-pro league in doubles one season as the result of being thrown out numerous times at third base trying to "stretch them out."

go. This step is important, because travel on the team bus is strictly controlled.

The bus was ready to leave the clubhouse in the middle of the afternoon. Since it was the last game of the season, players were already packed to leave for home when we returned from Durham, and lockers were almost cleaned out. Packing for the Durham trip was easy—uniforms, bats, gloves, and the clothes on your back. Of course there were also the CDs, magazines, food and entertainment items that must always accompany any sports team. This was a day trip with no overnight baggage needed, so the bus was light and so was the mood of the team.

But protocol is very important and starts with the seating arrangement. The manager is always on the front seat at the door, the pitching coach across the aisle, the other coaches and trainers behind them, and then the visitors and players. The team seating begins with those who want to listen to music, read or just sit, followed by those who play cards, talk or sleep during the ride. Conversation is lively, sometimes even about baseball, but on this trip it was mainly about going home and getting ready for the off-season.

The hour-and-a-half ride to Durham goes by fast. I sat with Matt Diehl of the Warthogs radio crew on the way down, and we talked about baseball. Before we knew it the bus was pulling into the Visitors entrance at the new Durham Bulls Athletic Park, and we were headed into the tunnel to the dressing room. The Durham facilities are top notch, and the players were greeted with sandwiches, drinks and a visiting clubhouse attendant ready to help them with any problem. The team dressed quickly and headed to the field for warm-ups and infield practice. There was no batting practice today.

Pre-game activities take a little longer tonight because it is the last Carolina League game for the Bulls (the two teams have been rivals in this league for the better part of 50 years). The Warthogs are attentive, but it is obvious they want to play ball. Jason Secoda warms up to pitch, and Carlos Lee is pacing the dugout talking to himself about the batting title that is on the line tonight and probably trying to jinx Rick Short of Frederick, who is just points ahead of him. The Warthogs front office staff is in the third row behind the dugout, the Booster Club members are down the third base line. "PLAY BALL" is called, and for the next three hours and 14 minutes all is right with the world and the 8479 fans who are a part of history.

The game was great. Ten innings and a 6–4 come-from-behind win for the Warthogs. Secoda, Jon Hunt and Chad Bradford combine for the win. Carlos Lee goes 3–5, hits his 50th double, scores a run and ends the season at .317, two percentage points behind Short. In the process he breaks three bats and has everyone wondering if we will have enough to finish the game. Fireworks follow the game, but the Warthogs take a quick shower, change clothes, put the equipment on the bus and head back down I-40 for Winston-Salem. They do take time for pizza and drinks, and pause for a minute to hear that Princess Diana has been injured in a wreck in Paris but will be okay.

Now it's time to push the bus driver for all he's worth. The trip home is hilarious, and Mark Haley wisely sits back and lets the team enjoy the moment. The next hour and a half could have been videotaped and replayed at a comedy club. Pitcher Jim Dixon leads the cheers and the fun, while everyone else lets the bus driver know we are going too slow. The classic line of the trip: "Ladies and gentlemen, we would like to announce that the bus has been passed by a parked car!" The bus driver is unaffected, citing the traffic laws and speed limits, and even rejecting offers of money and legal help in case he is arrested.

Near Greensboro a new chant starts. It begins with the name of the player, that he will return next year, and some interesting fact. Mark Haley is first. "Hales will return next year, and this time he'll have calves" (referring to Mark's slender lower legs). "Hasler will return, but this time with hair." Strength coach Don Toddings gets the treatment because of his GQ good looks and his perfectly cut hair. Trainer Scott Takao is pictured as the Samurai warrior who is out to get all of them. And so it goes, good natured, full of fun and typical of young men who have just finished a 140-game season.

One serious note. Near Winston-Salem, pitching coach Curt Hasler gets up and goes back to sit with Jason Secoda. The conversation is about the season, about pitching, about tonight's game and about the future. They are sitting just behind me so I can hear what is said, but true to the code, I will never repeat a word. But as I listen to Hasler's baseball knowledge pour out, I realize again that the minor leagues are truly the purest form of baseball left.

We pull into the clubhouse, the bus empties quickly and the players hurry to turn in equipment, clean out their lockers and collect their travel money or plane tickets from Pete Fisch. One event occurs I will never forget. Ann Haley, Mark's wife, is there and she tells us that Princess Diana has died in Paris from her injuries. As we watch TV in the manager's office, the night takes on a different historical significance and makes us all sad.

After 2:00 a.m. the players are gone, Scott is still inventorying equipment, the Haleys and Curt Hasler are ready to go, and Pete and I leave the clubhouse. A truly memorable night is over, and so is the last bus trip to Durham.

The Smallest of Them All

by Chris Holaday

While minor league baseball has been played all across the country in hundreds of towns of all sizes, one North Carolina town has the distinction of probably being the smallest of all.

As cities in North Carolina experienced dramatic growth during the early years of the 20th century, it opened the way for professional baseball to become a commercially viable form of entertainment. Charlotte, Greensboro and other larger cities were the first to field financially successful teams. Medium sized cities such as Rocky Mount and Goldsboro soon followed. As minor league baseball grew in popularity it became a matter of pride for towns to have a team to call their own, and by the 1930s professional baseball teams were being formed in towns like Ayden, Mayodan and Leaksville. Of all of these, the Greene County town of Snow Hill was the smallest.

The Snow Hill Billies were formed as a charter member of the Coastal Plain League in 1934. Other league members were Kinston, Greenville, New Bern, Ayden, and Tarboro. Goldsboro and Williamston were added to the lineup in 1935. Classified as semi-pro, the league teams were composed primarily of college players, very similar to the current Coastal Plain

---

Dallas, Texas, native Chris Holaday first discovered minor league baseball while a student at the University of North Carolina. Friends took him to a Durham Bulls game and he hasn't been the same since.

League which was formed in 1997. Pitcher Bob Bowman, who made it to the major leagues, played for the Billies in their semi-pro days. In 1937 the league decided to join the National Association, the governing organization of minor league baseball, and become a truly professional circuit. The Coastal Plain League was assigned the classification of D, the lowest level of pro baseball.

Owned by prominent local businessman and farmer Josiah Exum, the Billies were able to obtain a working agreement with the New York Yankees. This meant that the Yankees would supply a few players and have the first chance to purchase the contract of any other promising youngsters the Billies might sign. Unlike today, where the major league club pays the salaries of all players in its minor league system, most minor league teams were independent and made a large part of their money by selling players to the major leagues.

That first year as true professionals the Billies played great baseball and won the regular season pennant with a record of 62–36. In the playoffs they beat New Bern in the first round and then took the championship by defeating Tarboro, four games to one. The stars of the team that season were pitcher Emil Zak (16–3) and outfielder Dwight Wall (.279), the league leader in runs, with 88. Future major leaguer Aaron Robinson played third base and led the Billies with a .372 batting average and 85 RBIs. Manager D.C. "Peahead" Walker was also the Elon College football coach, later serving in that same role at Wake Forest College. Another notable member of the team was shortstop Walter Rabb (.242), who went on to spend 30 years as head baseball coach at the University of North Carolina.

The Billies fell to third place for the 1938 season (although they were only one game out of first) with a record of 61–49. They won in the first round of the playoffs, defeating Tarboro four games to two, but were swept in the finals by New Bern, four games to none. Pitcher Allen Gettel, in his first year of pro baseball, compiled a 16–7 record on his way to pitching in 184 major league games over seven seasons. Third baseman Tony Maisano was the team's leading offensive player, batting .354 with 78 RBIs, while Walter Rabb, in his second year as a Billie, hit .308. Catcher Jim Tatum, who batted .282, had been a star football player at UNC. He would later coach at the University of Oklahoma and at the University of Maryland, leading that school to a national championship in 1953.

In 1939 the Billies finished in a disappointing seventh place, winning 56 games and losing 64. It was not due to a lack of hitting, however, as catcher Joe Bistroff (.291, 108 RBIs) led the league in home runs with 32,

and Tony Maisano (.303) and first baseman Harry Soufas (.338, 30 HR, 104 RBIs) were both named to the All-Coastal Plain Team.

As the 1940 season approached, owner Josiah Exum informed town residents that the team had lost money and the only way baseball could continue in Snow Hill was if night baseball was implemented. This would allow more fans to attend the games since they wouldn't have to leave early from work to do so. The only problem was, Exum told them, he couldn't afford to pay for ballpark lights.

It appeared for awhile that Snow Hill's foray into the world of professional baseball was at an end. Thanks to fund-raising drives held by baseball boosters in the town, however, Exum decided to go ahead with the purchase of lights. He informed the league on April 2 that the town would field a team.

With the Opening Day scheduled for April 25, the Snow Hill club had a lot of catching up to do, and the ballpark was given a much-needed renovation. Exum put in a new outfield fence (which was moved back several feet), and the 1000-seat grandstand was basically rebuilt. What was referred to in the local paper as a "six-foot knoll that extended from second base to the right-center field fence" was graded level, and of course a new lighting system was installed. Exum and his staff were ready for the season, but the fact that fewer than 500 fans showed up for the opener did not bode well for the financial fortunes of the team.

On the field that season the Billies' performance was up and down. Shortstop Walter Rabb (.270, league-leading 428 assists), in his fourth season with the club, made the All-Coastal Plain Team, as did catcher Norm McCaskill (.272). First baseman L.D. Burdette was among the league leaders, with a .342 batting average, and the Billies' mound corps featured Bill Moran (15–9) and Virgil Taylor (17–12). Though they had some outstanding players, the team lacked depth, and in the end the best they could manage was a fifth-place, 62–64 finish.

It was obvious that the club had struggled financially, and after the season there were rumors that it would be sold. The fact that owner Exum had sold the lighting system to Elon College to help pay the bills was an ominous sign that days were numbered for the Snow Hill Billies. The end came in March of 1941 when the Billies franchise (which included

Opposite: The 1937 Snow Hill Billies. *Back:* John "Whack" Hyder, George Hruska, Joe Bertram, Joe "Jabber" Joyce. *Middle:* Gene "White Tie" McCann (Yankees scout), Emil Zak, Walter Latham, Dwight Hall, D.C. "Peahead" Walker. *Front:* Aaron Robinson, Harry Soufas, Horace Mewborn, Walter Rabb, Joe Bistroff. (Photograph courtesy of Walter Rabb.)

14 players and the team bus) was sold to a group of Rocky Mount businessmen for $2,100. The team was promptly relocated to that town, end-
ing Snow Hill's brief, yet unique, involvement with professional baseball.

With a population of only around 900 in 1940, Snow Hill is almost
certainly the smallest town in the entire nation to have ever had professional baseball. This is a difficult fact to establish, since many small towns,
Snow Hill included, were not incorporated, and populations were only
estimates. However, no other small minor league towns appear to have
had less than 1,500 residents. Despite the population, Snow Hill's Billies
often drew well over 1,500 fans to their games, attesting to the popularity of baseball in small North Carolina towns.

Nothing is left of the ballpark today; the site next to Contentnea
Creek has been overgrown for years. Time has erased all vestiges of the
place where local boys, as well as New York Yankees prospects, played the
game they loved, hoping for a chance to reach the big leagues.

Shoeless

by Thomas K. Perry

Joseph Jefferson Jackson walked with his father, brothers and sisters to Brandon Mill, where his job was to sweep the floors. Childhood was short, formal schooling nearly nonexistent, and by the age of six or seven children were following their parents into the noise and lint of the mill. Joe worked the long, boring hours, kept away from the freedom of the outdoors, but played pick-up baseball games with other children during their scheduled work breaks. He and his friends sometimes found chances to sneak away from their tasks for a while and play a few innings. The older workers may not have approved of such antics, but there was no denying his extraordinary grace as he galloped after fly balls and swung full and fluid from the left side of the plate.

By age thirteen, the boy was a regular on the Brandon men's team. He threw harder, ran faster and hit with more power than anyone could remember. His home runs were "Saturday Specials," since most textile games were scheduled after that half-day of work. Joe's brothers used to pass the hat after one of his round trippers, and Jackson seldom wanted for spending money, especially after leading Brandon to victories like the

A freelance writer living in Newberry, South Carolina, Tom Perry is the author of Textile League Baseball: South Carolina's Mill Teams, 1880–1955, *published by McFarland in 1993. His next project is an historical novel on the life of Joe's beloved wife, Katie Jackson.*

21–0 bombing of Anderson Mill in May of 1904. The line drives he hit were labeled "blue darters," which fielders and spectators swore crackled and smoked as they went by.

Not one to take his work tools lightly, Jackson supervised the making of his bat by a local craftsman. Weighing 48 ounces and lacquered with uncounted coats of tobacco juice, "Black Betsy" accompanied him during his baseball career. A favorite cheer of the fans became, "Give 'em Black Betsy, Joe!"

Jackson always had a bit of the showman in him and wanted to please the folks who came to watch him. After making a catch for the last out of a game, he would run to the deepest part of the outfield, turn at the fence and throw the ball on a line over the distant backstop behind home plate. Fans called such demonstrations "Showouts" and loved him for it. The strong arm and a glove "where triples go to die" were two more weapons in the arsenal of a wonderfully gifted athlete.

By age 19 Jackson was a legend in the Upstate area of South Carolina. He went from Brandon to Victor Mill in Greer, accepting a better offer to play baseball. While there, he was spotted by members of the semi-professional Greenville Near Leaguers, was signed and played with them briefly. His first professional stint came in 1908 with manager Tommy Stouch and the Greenville Spinners of the South Atlantic League. Though respectable middle class society marveled at his athletic ability, they hatefully ridiculed his cotton mill upbringing and his illiteracy. In their eyes, he was a worthless mill worker making the extraordinary salary of $75 a month.

Big league scouts were soon in attendance at his games, deciding for themselves whether this mill hill kid could live up to all they had heard about him. Jackson did not disappoint them, and his journey through organized baseball began. From Greenville he went to Connie Mack's Philadelphia Athletics, to minor league stints in Savannah and New Orleans, on to the Cleveland Indians, and finally settled in with Charles Comiskey's Chicago White Sox.

All the while his considerable talents were honed to near razor-sharp perfection, and his peers recognized him as a true professional. Detroit's Ty Cobb called Jackson the finest natural hitter the game ever saw. The Yankees' Babe Ruth modeled his swing after Joe's own, maintaining that he copied the best swing he could find. And Washington's Walter Johnson said "Shoeless" was the greatest natural ballplayer he ever competed against. "I gave him my best stuff," The Big Train would say, "and then go back up third base."

Jackson had good years with the Sox and played on their World

Championship team in 1917. But it was for his part played—or not played—in throwing the 1919 World Series that he is best remembered. He and seven teammates, found innocent in a trial by jury in 1921, nevertheless were banished for life from organized baseball by newly appointed commissioner Judge Kenesaw Mountain Landis.

Jackson's statistics for the Series underscored his greatness, without a hint of playing to lose: a leading batting average of .375; a record twelve hits (which stood for forty years); the leader in total bases and slugging percentage; the leading outfielder, with no errors and five runners gunned down on the base paths; and possessor of the Series' only home run.

Robert Ripley felt it only fair to include Jackson's incredible performance in his *Believe It or Not* collection. Surely, no one with such numbers could be accused of playing to lose. But Landis' ruling stood, and "Shoeless" never played another game in major league baseball.

He returned to Greenville in the autumn of 1920 for a visit, but continued on to Savannah with Lefty Williams, former teammate and another of the eight men out. Jackson opened a successful dry cleaning business and played ball from Bastrop, Louisiana, to Waycross, Georgia, and all points in between. His home state beckoned, and in 1929 he and his wife Katie returned to Greenville to open another dry cleaning store. Later, a barbecue house (with the first curb service offered in the area) and a liquor store were added to his list of successful entrepreneurial ventures. The hero had returned. Jackson was home, and mill village citizens looked after their own.

His ties with textile baseball were never really broken, and he made himself available to the players, working with and encouraging them. Brandon's Murphy Grumbles was so determined to prove his mentor right that he earned a standout reputation during his years in the mill leagues. Joe was also the yardstick against whom all players were measured. Pel Ballenger of Judson, George Blackwell of Southern Bleachery, and even younger brother Jerry Jackson of Woodside Mill were but a few who understood the burdens of such a comparison.

In 1935 Jackson managed the Winnsboro, SC, team, then moved to Woodside Mill in 1938 and played on the same team with his brother Jerry. He was the recognized celebrity, drawing the most cheers during the 1937 King Cotton League opener when introduced as a member of the 1907 Victor Mill team, which won 19 straight games against stiff competition. Jackson made it to the 1939 Eastern Carolina League/Western Carolina League All-Star Game, batting for both teams in the third inning. Showing no favoritism, he rifled out a double in each plate appearance. He played regularly until well into his forties and pinch-hit in a mill league

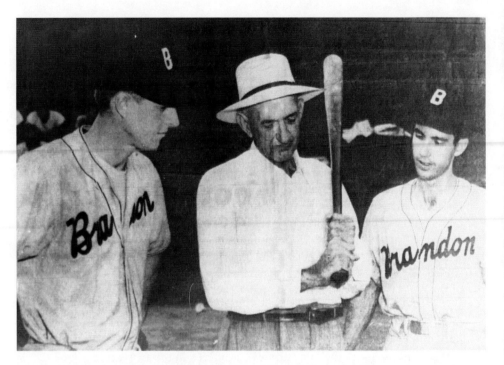

Brandon Mill players Ralph Harbin (left) and Harry Foster (right) receiving advice from Joe Jackson in 1948. (Photograph courtesy of Joe Anders.)

game at age 56. Already weakened by the first of three heart attacks, he smashed the ball off the centerfield fence, 415 feet from home plate.

There have been many attempts to clear the reputation of "Shoeless" Joe Jackson. The South Carolina Legislature adopted a formal resolution in 1951, calling for his reinstatement into organized baseball. Baseball Commissioner Happy Chandler was involved in another effort on Joe's behalf. None of these succeeded.

Death came calling December 5, 1951, and brought rest to the man whose life was overshadowed by events of an autumn classic 30 years before. Perhaps he was innocence personified, swept away by forces he could neither understand nor fight. Whatever the reasons, the legend of "Shoeless" Joe has grown to near mythic proportions.

Jackson always denied any truth to the story of the little boy clutching at his sleeve and pleading, "Say it ain't so, Joe! Say it ain't!" as players were leaving that Chicago courtroom in 1921. For those who knew him from his days on the mill village, from his "Saturday Specials" to his "Showouts," he never had to say it wasn't so. The folks who knew him best never questioned his integrity, and gave back to him the assurance that the legend would never die.

Joe Jackson continues to challenge our collective conscience. There is another campaign underway to have his name removed from baseball's list of ineligible players. Spearheaded by Hall of Fame members Ted Williams and Tommy Lasorda, this group contends that Jackson served his lifetime banishment with dignity, and that his name should be cleared. This would allow him to be considered for election into the National Baseball Hall of Fame. To date, Commissioner Bud Selig has not ruled on the petition.

Tribute to a Ballpark

by Marshall Adesman

Can you write a love letter to a building, especially one that doesn't see much use any more and doesn't look quite like it used to? I suppose you can, since other edifices have been sources of inspiration before—"Give me your tired, your poor, your huddled masses…" comes to mind. Durham Athletic Park, therefore, is the subject of this tribute.

Not the new ballyard, mind you, but the old one, the traditional one. There's nothing really wrong with the current facility, aside from its unimaginative name of Durham Bulls Athletic Park. Made of brick and wrought iron, it was designed as one of those modern "retro" parks, a structure like Baltimore's Camden Yards that pays homage to the early 20th century baseball facilities that were inner city centerpieces and helped to spread the popularity of professional baseball. Constructed in downtown Durham as part of an ongoing effort to resurrect the business district, it holds about 10,000 fans and offers them comfortable seats (with cup holders!), plenty of leg room, wide concourses and a great variety of food, drink and amusements. It also features Triple-A baseball as the Bulls, formerly in the Class A Carolina League, have moved up to the minor leagues' highest classification. In short, this new ballpark, opened in 1995,

In his travels Marshall Adesman has visited dozens of minor league ballparks across the country. Though he appreciates modern amenities, generally the older and more quirky a ballpark is, the more he likes it.

offers every possible amenity to its numerous visitors. Except charm, which the old park had in abundance.

After working in baseball as assistant general manager in Amarillo, Texas, and general manager in Waterloo, Iowa, I was familiar with old ballparks, and at first blush the DAP (the shorthand adopted for old Durham Athletic Park) seemed no different. But that was in February, and you can't really gauge the tenor of a yard until the dogs are hot, the beer is cold and the fans are exhorting the team to score one more run.

Like so many towns across the nation, the history of minor league ball in Durham mirrored the social conditions of America. They became members of the Piedmont League in 1920 and stayed there for fourteen seasons as the loop advanced from Class D to Class C to Class B during the "Roaring Twenties." Durham dropped out for two years during the Great Depression but returned in 1936. The then-new Durham

The unique ticket booth at Durham Athletic Park. (Photograph courtesy of Chris Holaday.)

Athletic Park opened in 1939 and hosted Piedmont League action until 1944, the height of World War II, when only ten minor leagues operated and no city in North Carolina was able to field a team. But in 1945 the war was winding down and the Bulls were back, this time in the Class C Carolina League, and they stayed there through 1967 and the league's ascendance to Class B and then Class A. The minor leagues, however, suffered in the 1950s and 1960s: From a high of 59 leagues and 438 franchises in 1949, only 15 minor leagues and 118 cities suited up in 1965. A booming post-war economy allowed Americans to buy their own homes in the suburbs, away from inner-city based teams. Automobiles were now affordable and could go farther on the new high-speed interstate highways. And when people stayed at home they found new comfort as window air-conditioners brought indoor relief from the summertime heat, allowing families to watch those new television sets. From 1968 through 1971, in an effort to survive, the neighboring cities of Raleigh and Durham combined their teams into one, with home games played in both towns. But fans in the area couldn't get excited about this split-city concept and continued to stay away; after four years, the experiment quietly ended as professional baseball left the Triangle region of North Carolina.

The turbulence of the 1960s and early 1970s—symbolized first by the fight for civil rights and then by the war in Vietnam and its accompanying protests—finally subsided following the end of the Watergate crisis and Richard Nixon's 1974 resignation. And within a couple of years the recovering nation re-discovered minor league baseball. Jim Paul painted Dudley Field a bright red and yellow, instituted a series of crazy promotions, and turned a dying franchise in El Paso into the bellwether of the Texas League. George Sisler, Jr., convinced Franklin County to refurbish their old ballpark as Columbus, Ohio, returned to the professional ranks after a six-year hiatus and drew a minor-league high 457,000 fans. And Vanderbilt baseball coach Larry Schmittou successfully brought minor league ball back to Nashville after a fifteen-year absence. Young urban professionals, remembering how they had gone to the ballpark with their parents, and now motivated by a variety of creative promotional efforts, started bringing their own children out to root, root, root for the home team.

The economic boom really hit North Carolina's Piedmont. Formerly ruled by tobacco, the area was transformed by the development of the Research Triangle Park, originally used by the three major universities (Duke, North Carolina and North Carolina State), then expanded to include government agencies and private businesses. Northerners and Midwesterners were transferred in, and as they settled down they looked for things to do. Miles Wolff, a career baseball man and a North Carolinian by birth, recognized that the area was very different at the end of the 1970s than it had been at the beginning. He also saw how absence can make a city's heart grow fonder: In addition to the above examples of Columbus and Nashville, there was also Greensboro, just 54 miles west, which had made a triumphal return to professional baseball after an eleven-year gap by posting the highest attendance among Class A league teams. So when the Carolina League decided to expand, Wolff chose to operate a franchise in Durham for the 1980 season. The result exceeded all expectations, as nearly 176,000 fans streamed into the small downtown ballpark. A legend was born. (*Editor's note:* See Miles Wolff's story about the 1980 Bulls, pages 137–149.)

What these "cranks" found was a ballpark just oozing personality out of every pore.* When fans walked up to the ticket window they found the three sellers housed in the ground floor of a rounded tower that seemed more appropriate for Rapunzel than for a baseball park. Rather than a fair maiden, the tower was home to the Bulls' business operations, and from the top of the winding staircase I, as business manager, would look down and see most of the bustling facility.

Built like a bowl, you entered at the old girl's apex and descended to points east and west. Traversing the narrow concourses was generally done slowly and single-file, but it gave everyone a chance to examine the culinary diversity. One concession stand specialized in a variety of burritos, while another offered either nachos or a chicken sandwich. Down the first-base ramp and behind the bleachers was a wonderful stand that sold hamburgers, cheeseburgers, the best french fries this side of Maryland's Eastern Shore, and a variety of other higher-priced fare. Snack items could be found in a small stand tucked away on the third-base side, and several stations around the park sold a variety of beers. And it was all tied together by the main concession stand, just a few feet from the base of the tower. It was basically the first thing you saw as you entered the park and it offered standard ballpark fare like hot dogs, popcorn, peanuts, soft drinks and ice cream, in addition to pizza. It was also (along with the first-base beer stand) the primary place for socializing, the place for friends to meet, grab their grub and find their seats. A beer stand and souvenir stand were also located there, and on busy nights this general area looked like a miniature version of Times Square (minus the XXX-rated theaters).

Oh, Jay also lived there. I don't recall his last name but he was the loud-voiced young man who hawked programs just beyond the main entrance. Everyone knew Jay because he made it his business to get to know you and give you his opinion on any and all topics. Jay was a die-hard Braves fan, which took a lot of guts through much of the 1980s, but

---

Not everyone recognized the old park's attributes. The aforementioned Larry Schmittou had looked at Durham when he and his partners decided to put a team in the South Atlantic League. After a tour of the DAP, Schmittou told city officials that the park ought to have a bomb dropped on it, and opted instead for Greensboro. More than twenty years later, it is worth noting that the Bulls' success in the old ballpark spawned the construction of the new facility and their ascendance to Triple-A. Greensboro, on the other hand, remains in the South Atlantic League and has been unsuccessful in garnering any assistance to replace its deteriorating, septuagenarian stadium, and Larry Schmittou is no longer active in professional baseball.

he correctly observed that Atlanta, our parent club, was sending us some good players who would eventually surface in the majors and make the Braves a better team. And with the infusion of such players as Steve Avery, Jeff Blauser, Ron Gant, David Justice and Mark Lemke, Atlanta made its astounding run from last place in 1990 to the World Series in 1991. Other Bulls alumni, such as Chipper Jones, Ryan Klesko, Javy Lopez and Andruw Jones, continued the Braves' success throughout the 1990s. I'm sure Jay has enjoyed every minute of it ... and hasn't been shy about sharing his feelings with others.

If you had box or reserved seats (no luxury boxes in this Depression-era edifice), you walked past Jay and the main concession stand (and also past the door leading to the small administrative offices) and descended down the stairs. Capacity was around 5,000, but very often more than 1,000 other fans were shoehorned in. The covered grandstand could hold upwards of 3,000, and the rest found refuge in the backless bleacher seats along the first or third-base lines, or sometimes on the grass beyond the centerfield fence. For some reason the rowdiest fans were almost always found along third base—they not only seemed to enjoy the game a little more, but they also took particular delight in heckling the opposition and baiting the umpires. They certainly had a better view of the field than the denizens of the press box, which was literally a box built at field level right behind home plate. Popups and high flies immediately disappeared from sight, and the official scorer, PA announcer and assorted writers had to watch the players to determine who was chasing the ball.

The dugouts were small, as befitting a facility built when both rosters and athletes were smaller. The playing field itself was also, um, cozy, with its rightfield line famous throughout the league as an inviting target. It was publicly listed as 305 feet, but that was definitely an exaggeration. Miles once told me they had actually measured it at about 291 feet, but knew that Organized Baseball would object to such a short porch and thus they simply didn't publicize the true distance. A side wall of a local business sat just a few feet beyond that rightfield fence, thankfully made of brick because many a blast smashed against it over the course of a summer. In 1984, my first year in Durham, we had a big first baseman named Bob Tumpane, a lefthanded pull hitter who must have played pepper with that wall about twenty times.

After that scintillating 1980 debut, attendance declined somewhat for the next three seasons, bottoming out at 142,000 in 1983. While still very respectable, six other teams in Class A topped it, including fellow Carolina League member Hagerstown. But Wolff promoted Assistant General Manager Rob Dlugozima after the 1983 season, and Dlugozima led

The venerable old grandstand. (Photograph courtesy of Chris Holaday.)

the team into a period of unprecedented growth, cementing the Bulls' status as one of minor league baseball's elite franchises. After just missing in 1986, attendance soared beyond 200,000 in 1987, and then Hollywood stepped in.

Thom Mount had grown up in Durham and his family still owned season tickets at the DAP. When a former ballplayer, Ron Shelton, brought him a story fashioned around a minor league team, Mount—now a Hollywood producer—thought of shooting it in his hometown. Production started right after the 1987 season ended and lasted for several weeks, with a few scenes also shot in Greensboro and Asheville. The following spring *Bull Durham*, featuring Kevin Costner, Susan Sarandon and Tim Robbins, opened to extremely positive reviews, and suddenly the Durham Athletic Park was a star in its own right. People came from all over the country to sit in the ballpark they had seen on the big screen. Attendance jumped to 271,000 in 1988 and 300,000 in 1990.

There is always a price to pay, of course. While the team was making tons of money and receiving international recognition, the park was bulging at the seams. It had not been designed for that kind of high-volume usage, and, now more than fifty years old, it was rapidly showing its age. It soon became apparent that either a major facelift or a brand-new facility was needed in the Bull City. The ensuing political battle took several years, led to a change in ownership, involved several neighboring counties as well as members of baseball's inner circle, and is discussed elsewhere in this volume. However, it was determined that a completely new park was the most cost-effective solution, and in 1995 the Durham Bulls Athletic Park opened and drew nearly 400,000 fans. Three years later, after 18 seasons as the Braves' affiliate in the Carolina League, the Bulls became the Triple-A farm club of the expansion Tampa Bay Devil Rays, where they maintain their status as one of the minor leagues' most successful franchises.

So everyone is happy, right? Well, not quite. Perhaps I am the only one who still misses the old DAP, now shorn of its bleachers but still used for some high school games and a collegiate summer league, as well as a farmer's market on weekends. The new ballpark is great and I certainly appreciate it, but it's just a building. I know I have said this before, but the Durham Athletic Park had its own special personality, charm and vitality, qualities I find lacking in its successor. I still enjoy going to the ballgame, of course, but I'm sorry, there's just something missing, something that can never be recaptured. A victim of her own success, the Grand Dame now lives primarily in the hearts of those who still love her, who still remember when a ballpark was a ballpark and not a stadium.

Think I'll go downtown and sit in the grandstand, where I can close my eyes and still smell the popcorn being popped. Plenty of room, feel free to join me.

A Gaylord Perry Story

by Parker Chesson

The year 1958 was a big one for bonus babies coming out of North Carolina high schools. Tony Cloninger from Lincoln County and Gaylord Perry from Martin County signed large bonus contracts within a few weeks of each other. Just two years earlier, Perry's older brother Jim had signed for only $4,000 under the rule that at that time required players signing contracts for more than $4,000 to be kept on the major league team's roster. This rule was dropped in 1957, however, allowing Cloninger and Gaylord Perry to get into bidding contests for their services. Cloninger signed with the Milwaukee Braves for a bonus reported to be close to $100,000. The younger Perry was signed in June 1958 for a bonus and three years of salary totaling $73,500, the most the Giants had ever paid a rookie.

Gaylord had a phenomenal high school career, starring in baseball, football, and basketball. I attended Perquimans County High School, which gave me the "opportunity" to compete against Gaylord, since it was

Dr. Parker Chesson recently retired after a 36-year career in public service. He served as president of the College of the Albemarle from 1975 to 1992, executive vice president of the North Carolina Community College System from 1992 to 1996, and chairman of the Employment Security Commission of North Carolina from 1996 to 2000. A native of Hertford, North Carolina, he now lives in Durham, North Carolina.

Ah, the cockiness of youth: the young hurler from Perquimans County. (Photograph courtesy of Parker Chesson.)

in the same conference as Williamston High School. Gaylord, who was a year older than me, and I were both pitchers who played other positions when not on the mound. Unfortunately, the similarities pretty much stopped there.

I remember our encounters with Williamston High School, especially the ones when Gaylord was on the mound. At 6'4" and about 200 pounds, he was an imposing figure, and he had a blazing fastball. Talent wise, he was in another league. During the spring of 1958 the weather was unusually wet and cool, and Gaylord, in his autobiography *Me and the Spitter,* says he held back to protect his arm. His record of 7–2 was not as good as in previous seasons and his team did not get far in the state playoffs.

One game I especially recall was played on April 1, 1958, when Gaylord was scheduled to pitch at Memorial Field behind Perquimans County High School. This is the same ballpark in which the late Jim "Catfish" Hunter played his high school games. Amazingly, that pitcher's mound, which is in the same location today, has seen two Hall of Famers pitch off of it.

I had the rather unenviable task of pitching against Gaylord on that April day when he was a senior and I was a junior. There was a lot of talk leading up to that game, including the fact that many major league scouts were supposed to attend. Our school principal, Mr. Woodard, stopped me in the hall that morning and told me he had gotten calls from several major league scouts asking for directions and other information. He really got my attention when he said, "Maybe this will be a chance to show your stuff." Needless to say, that did nothing to calm my nerves.

I still have a mental picture of the scene behind home plate that day as our fans slowly filed into the ballpark. Early in the season during those days we played our home games during school hours, starting at about two o'clock. This allowed students to attend the games. Those riding school buses would have to leave early, but at least they got to see the first few innings. On that day, the seats behind home plate contained many men I had never laid eyes on before, some of them quite old from my perspective as a 16-year-old boy. Obviously, they were scouts, and it looked like a whole busload of them. Almost all of the major league teams had been actively scouting Gaylord. I noticed that a motion picture camera was even set up behind the screen and slightly to the right of

The Pride of Williamston: Gaylord Perry as a San Francisco Giant. (Photograph courtesy of Chris Holaday.)

home plate so that it would get a good view of the pitcher during his windup and delivery.

Mr. Woodard's earlier conversation with me flashed through my mind as I went out to the mound in the top of the first inning for my warm up tosses. Now would be my chance. Pitch a good game, get recorded on that film, and maybe, just maybe, they would remember me as well as Gaylord Perry.

My hope quickly vanished. I noticed in the first inning and throughout the game that the man who bent over and squinted through the camera's viewer was there only when Williamston was in the field and Gaylord was on the mound. When I was pitching, he would sit back down among the scouts or go off to get a drink. Obviously, his behavior was the result of one of two things—either they did not have much film in that camera or they were not interested in the pitcher for Perquimans County High School!

The game turned out to be a good one, and the Raleigh *News & Observer* reported the next day in a short write-up, "Perry struck out 15 and walked one in besting Hertford's Chesson in a tight pitching duel. Each allowed four hits, and Chesson fanned four." Bev Tucker, one of my best friends and a classmate throughout my school years, hit a triple off Gaylord that day. He reminds me of that whenever we start reminiscing about our high school days. How many former high school players can say they once hit a triple off a Hall of Fame pitcher?

But let me finish my story. I later learned it was the San Francisco Giants that had set up the camera behind home plate that day. For that game, Tom Sheehan, the Giants' chief scout and close associate of team owner Horace Stoneham, had been flown in from San Francisco to watch. As reported by the *News & Observer*, after watching five innings, Sheehan told area scout Tim Murchison, "You better make arrangements to sign that boy." Murchison, with the assistance of fellow scout Earl Smith, did just that and Gaylord Perry became a Giant.

After a couple of seasons in the minors, Gaylord made his debut for the big league club in 1962. Developing into one of the National League's most dominant pitchers of the late '60s, he won 134 games for the Giants over 10 seasons, and topped the 20-win mark in both 1966 and 1970. His big-league career would eventually span 22 seasons, during which he played for eight different clubs and won 314 games. Elected to the National Baseball Hall of Fame in 1991, Gaylord is the only pitcher to win the coveted Cy Young Award in both leagues, and his 3534 strikeouts put him sixth on the all-time list.

After retiring from the playing field, Gaylord Perry didn't remain away from baseball for long. In 1988 he founded the baseball program at Limestone College in Gaffney, South Carolina, and served as the school's head coach from 1988 to 1991.

Bobby Hipps

by Hank Utley

Robert Elwood Hipps was born in the small North Carolina mountain town of Canton, located not far from Asheville, in 1905. Like most boys, sports played a big part in his growing up, and he excelled in many of them. But, during his years in the local Canton schools and later at Oak Ridge Military Academy near Greensboro, baseball became young Bobby's true love. He displayed a talent that would keep him involved in that game for nearly half a century.

After high school Hipps enrolled at Weaver College near his hometown, but he was only there for a year before transferring to Furman University. At the South Carolina school Hipps had a stellar career and was named to the All-State baseball team in both 1925 and '26. His skills were not just limited to the diamond, as he received Honorable Mention on the All-State football team and even played a season of varsity basketball. As a senior in 1926, Hipps was elected captain of the baseball squad and

---

Hank Utley, after graduating from North Carolina State College and having given up active baseball participation, was working for Mooresville Mills in 1950. In late August he was informed by the company owner that he must help the mill-sponsored Mooresville Moors professional baseball team finish out the season since several players had been drafted for the Korean War. Not in shape, Hank defined what is known among ball players as the "stark-naked third baseman" for the many errors he made.

(thanks to a .435 batting average) was named Furman's most valuable player. For this honor he was awarded a full-size silver bat. These accomplishments did not go unnoticed; after graduating he was promptly signed by Connie Mack's Philadelphia Athletics.

Furman University's yearbook, the *Bonhomie*, had this to say about the star athlete: "Bob is a native of North Carolina who has brought fame to Furman. Because he brought credits from another college when he entered Furman he is able to finish in three years. He is a star athlete; one of the best football and basketball stars Furman has turned out in some years. In baseball, however, he has gained most of his glory. He has been for the past two years the best first baseman in South Carolina, and has already signed a contract with the Philadelphia Athletics to whom he will go as soon as he has the diploma tucked away. Last year he was voted the best looking man at the University; this fact, coupled with that neat little coupe that is at his disposal at all times, has served to make him the University Beau Brummel. If it is his will, and he has a strong one, we shall see him become one of the best first sackers in the major leagues."

Unfortunately, Hipps never would achieve the major league stardom predicted in the 1926 yearbook, but he did have a successful minor league career. Right after graduation the Philadelphia Athletics shipped him to Connecticut to begin his professional career with the Hartford Senators in the Class A Eastern League. Hipps played fairly well, hitting a respectable .270 in 39 games, but the big league club decided to see how he would do in the Class A Southern Association. Joining the Chattanooga Lookouts in mid-season, Hipps was given the chance for more playing time. He responded with an outstanding .339 batting average.

The 1927 season would also be split between two teams; for the first half Hipps was with Chattanooga before being sent to Asheville in the Class B South Atlantic League. In 1928 he was assigned to the Durham Bulls of the Class C Piedmont League, but an injury limited him to only 46 games.

During the off-seasons, beginning in the fall of 1927, Hipps worked in the Asheville area as a teacher and a coach at Weaverville and Grace High Schools. In 1934 he was hired as assistant baseball coach at Asheville's Edwards High School.

In 1929, at the age of 24, Hipps returned to play for the Asheville Tourists. For three consecutive seasons he would be the team's star first baseman, and with each year his numbers only got better. In 1931, as a result of the financial difficulties caused by the Great Depression, the South Atlantic League folded. Despite this, the Asheville Tourists wanted to continue play and were able to switch to the Class C Piedmont League.

Statistically, that would be the best season of Hipps' entire playing career, as he batted .360 and drove in 106 runs. For those three fantastic seasons it looked as if Bobby Hipps had finally matured into a true major-league caliber player, but the call from the big leagues never came.

For the 1932 season Hipps made a big geographical move by signing with the Tulsa Oilers of the Class A Western League. He played well and hit .289 as the Oilers won the league championship, sweeping the Oklahoma City Indians in the playoffs. The stay in Oklahoma would last only one season, though, as Hipps joined the Knoxville Smokies of the Class A Southern League for 1933.

It was back to Asheville for the 1934 season, but Hipps was soon on the move again. A month into the season he was headed north to Pennsylvania to join what would be his final club in organized professional baseball, the Class A Williamsport Grays. Hipps played a large part in that club's winning of the New York–Penn League Championship.

In 1935, at the age of 30, Bobby Hipps made a career changing decision that kept him in baseball for four more years and at the same time laid a foundation on which he built a business career. He dropped out of organized professional baseball and started playing for the Cooleemee Cools in the Carolina Textile League. Cooleemee was one of many villages in North Carolina built around a single textile mill. It joined Landis and Mooresville, also single-mill towns, and together with the slightly larger multiple-mill towns of Concord, Salisbury, and Kannapolis formed the Carolina Textile League. In this highly competitive league, Hipps was just one of many players with professional experience signed by member teams. In mid-season 1935, he switched teams and took over as a playing manager for Kannapolis. There, Hipps hit .342 and made the league All-Star team as first baseman.

During the winter of 1935-36 the Carolina Textile League reorganized and transformed itself into a completely professional league. Called the Carolina League, it operated outside the province of the National Association, minor league baseball's governing body, hence earning the title of an "outlaw" league. Players didn't complain though, since it offered more money and the year-round security of a job in the mills. The professional baseball establishment, on the other hand, tried to shut the league down and threatened to ban all players who appeared in it.

As the Carolina League members mounted one of the early challenges to baseball's reserve clause, Hipps and fellow player-managers Art Hord and Jim Poole could be found in the background giving advice and guidance to the textile mill owners and civic leaders. In reality they didn't challenge the reserve clause (which, in essence, stated players were the sole

Hipps (kneeling, far left) with his 1935 Kannapolis team. Pitcher Buck Ross (two players to Hipps' left) went on to play several years in the major leagues. (Photograph courtesy of Hank Utley.)

possession of the team they signed with until that team said otherwise) as much as they ignored it. It would be years later, in the 1970s, before professional players would finally successfully challenge the reserve clause in the courts of the United States.

After the collapse of the Carolina League at the end of the 1938 season, Bobby Hipps made his first move into business management. He was selected to be general manager of the Central Motor Lines in Lenoir, NC. The president of Central Motor Lines, Robert Hayes, was closely associated with Cannon Mills in Kannapolis. How a man only with experience managing baseball players could be named manager of a trucking company can be explained by a conversation businessman Cork Caldwell recalled that had taken place between Dick Rankin, a prominent doctor in the Kannapolis area, and Cannon Mills executive Alex Howard. He remembered Dr. Rankin saying, "Alex, I see where Bobby Hipps has been named General Manager of Central Motor Lines in Lenoir. What does that man know about managing a motor line? He's done nothing but play baseball all his life." Alex Howard replied, "For four years in the Carolina League, Bobby Hipps has shown leadership abilities and has proven he knows how to manage men. That type of man is hard to find. We can teach him the technical end of the trucking business but you cannot teach a man management skills on the job. Hipps knows how to manage men."

Though Hipps' playing career was over, his love of baseball was too great to keep him away from the game for long. From 1941 to 1947 he was a baseball scout, first for the Atlanta Crackers and then the Pittsburgh Pirates. In 1947 he resigned from the Pirates and went into the used car business in Asheville. Soon he became part owner of Sam's Motor Sales, the city's Lincoln and Mercury dealer. (He would retire as the company's vice president and treasurer in 1971.) Hipps was also a prominent civic leader, serving as commissioner of the Asheville Housing Authority.

Even while becoming a business leader in Asheville, Hipps couldn't stay away from his beloved game. In 1951 professional baseball called again when the presidency of the Tri-State League, a Class B circuit with teams in South Carolina, North Carolina, and Tennessee, was offered to him. Hipps eagerly accepted the job.

It is ironic that Bobby Hipps, a man who loved and gave so much to the game of baseball, would have to shoulder the pains of the demise that minor league baseball was going through in the early 1950s. The world of entertainment was changing, led by the growing television industry, and fans were not coming out to the ballparks in record numbers like they had just a few seasons before. For five years, from 1951 to 1955, Bobby Hipps

Bobby Hipps as a league president. (Photograph courtesy of Hank Utley.)

was a man possessed by optimism and drive, trying to save professional baseball in the region. In the end, however, it proved to be a fight that couldn't be won.

After Hipps died in 1980, Bob Terrell, sportswriter for the *Asheville Times*, wrote the following eulogy: "Hipps was league president for five years, until the league folded after the 1955 season. Had it not been for his efforts, his tireless work, and his many contacts in baseball, the league would have gone under a year or two before it did. I came to know Hipps as perhaps the most honest man I ever had to approach for a story. When you asked him a question, he gave a straight answer. He didn't beat around the bush, and he didn't try to hide anything. He was an optimist. He believed that through honest effort, he could hold the Tri-State League together. In 1954 and '55, when the league threatened every month to cave in, Hipps played every possible angle and held it together. I remember two headlines in the *Times*. One read 'Hipps Smiles While Tri-State Totters,' and the other, in February of 1955: 'Will It Take Miracle Work To Save Tri-State League Now?' Hipps saved it. Most of the cities had folded up but Hipps promoted a four-team league in 1955 consisting of Asheville, Spartanburg, Greenville, and Rock Hill, and played the entire season. At the end of the 1955 season, the league folded. Nothing, not even Bobby Hipps, could have saved it."

Baseball did eventually return to Asheville in the 1960s, but by that time Bobby Hipps' only official involvement with the game was as an avid fan. Unofficially, however, he still helped guide the careers of players and league presidents alike by sharing his years of experience. Even today, more than 20 years after his death, his contributions to the game he loved are not forgotten.

Bobby Hipps' complete playing record:

Year	Team	G	AB	R	H	2B	3B	HR	RBI	AVG
1926	Hartford	36	126	16	34	8	1	1	-	.270
	Chattanooga	39	124	21	42	4	3	2	-	.339
1927	Chattanooga	69	258	33	54	9	4	1	29	.248
	Asheville	84	312	31	79	15	6	2	-	.253
1928	Durham	46	164	17	42	5	2	0	15	.257
1929	Asheville	140	501	68	162	25	7	5	72	.323
1930	Asheville	134	534	105	184	26	11	3	78	.345
1931	Asheville	130	481	104	173	36	17	11	106	.360
1932	Tulsa	143	592	147	171	26	10	9	75	.289
1933	Knoxville	126	470	73	136	17	4	7	81	.289
1934	Asheville	18	56	4	10	2	1	0	5	.179
	Williamsport	96	354	47	92	22	1	6	59	.260
1935	Cooleemee/									
	Kannapolis	-	144	26	39	8	3	4	-	.342
1936	Concord	-	180	42	58	15	2	8	42	.322
1937	Concord	-	300	71	95	12	7	12	56	.317
1938	Lenoir	-	338	79	122	20	7	8	50	.361

Black Professional Baseball in North Carolina from World War I to the Depression

by Bijan C. Bayne

Before the establishment of the Negro National League and Eastern Colored League of the 1920s, black men were playing professional baseball all over North Carolina. From Wilmington on the eastern coast to Asheville in the Blue Ridge Mountains, black-owned ballclubs played a high level of baseball and developed many players who went on to the better known Negro leagues.

Black teams in North Carolina never received the attention that the major Negro league clubs of the North and Midwest did. Though they had many talented players, teams in the state (as well as much of the South) were often less organized and frequently did not play in organized leagues. Because of that, records were often not kept. In addition, the newspapers of the day gave little mention to these teams, and it was rare that box scores or game highlights ever made it to print.

Bijan C. Bayne is the author of Sky Kings: Black Pioneers of Professional Basketball. *He is a freelance writer in Cincinnati, Ohio.*

Following are a few bits of information about teams and players from the early days of black baseball in North Carolina:

• The Raleigh Black Star Line were a team named after Black Nationalist leader Marcus Garvey, who had a freight company called The Black Star Line. There were the Raleigh Tar Heels of 1920 and 1921. The Heels starred pitcher Eulace Harrington and catcher Bud Birch. Local fans used to compare Harrington's skills with the better-known "Satchel" Paige.
• Raleigh also had the Grays in 1919 and 1920. Their owner was a South Carolinian with the surname Scott. Grays players included catchers Allen Omstead and James Yancey, first baseman "Red" McCoy, second baseman C.D. Watkins, a shortstop named Taylor, third baseman Willard Perry, and outfielders Charles "Doll" Haywood and Fred Williams.
• Hall of Fame black shortstop-manager John Henry "Pop" Lloyd took an interest in the Raleigh Grays, thinking he could sign their pitcher "Red Top" Turner to the Bacharach Giants. Lloyd stayed in Raleigh to ensure that the team's practices were competitive because he saw the team as a talent base for his Giants. Red Top never went north to pitch, however; the Shaw College graduate enrolled in medical school.
• Walter "Buck" Leonard of Rocky Mount, NC, got his baseball start with his hometown team, the Rocky Mount Elks. The Elks became the Black Swans, and Leonard was a team regular in 1921 at age 14. The Swans, managed by Raymond Stith, played every black pro and semi-pro team within a 150-mile radius of Rocky Mount, including High Point, the Greensboro Black Patriots, the aforementioned Raleigh teams, the Winston-Salem Pond Giants and the Salisbury Red Sox. They also faced Statesville, Tarboro, Smithfield, and Durham's Black Sox. Opponents from other states included Florence, SC; the Richmond Giants (1922–23); Petersburg, VA; the Norfolk, VA, Stars; and Newport News, VA. Buck Leonard managed the Swans before he was 20 years old. Leonard became a longtime Homestead Grays first baseman and Baseball Hall of Fame inductee.
• Other out-of-town teams that faced black professional Carolinians were the 1924 Washington Potomacs, the Baltimore Black Sox, and the Portsmouth, VA, Firefighters. The competition was strong. Hall of Famer-to-be Ray Dandridge starred for Richmond, VA, in 1928.
• A few Tar Heel nines faced the 1919–1921 Norfolk (VA) Stars, who featured pitcher Nip Winters. Winters went on to pitch for the Hilldale Stars, for whom he beat Hall of Fame pitcher Lefty Grove and a team of Earl Mack's All Stars in 1926. George "Chappie" Johnson managed the

Norfolk club; he later skippered the Mohawk Giants of Schenectady. The Winston Salem Pond Giants played the Norfolk Stars in June of 1921. On June 13, 1921, the Edenton (NC) Giants lost to Norfolk. Among the Edenton players were Brown, two men named Revens, Hale, George, Scott, Jordan, Deasley, and Blunt.

• Edenton had another ballclub in 1921, the Braves. On September 26 of that year they hosted the Suffolk (VA) Sunbeams, who the Norfolk *Journal and Guide* newspaper called champions of the Tidewater region of Virginia (Portsmouth, Norfolk, Hampton, Newport News). Despite the prowess of the visiting Virginians, the *Journal and Guide* projected "a good game is expected."

• On July 18, 1921, 1,500 spectators saw the Elizabeth City (NC) Giants host the Norfolk Stars. The home team featured W. Winslow at first, H. McMuman on second, H. Hawkins at short, O. Glover playing third base, T. Glover catching, with an outfield of L.W. Smith in left, J. Slade in center, F. Barrington in right field.

• Dave "Skinny Green" Barnhill pitched for his hometown team in Greenville, NC, before going on to the Indianapolis Clowns and stardom in Puerto Rico. Burnelle "Bun" Hayes was a pitching ace in Louisburg, NC, prior to his days with the Baltimore Black Sox. The fireballing Hayes was one of several professional stars to emerge from Johnson C. Smith College in Charlotte.

• Leamon Yokely, out of Livingstone College in Salisbury, NC, tossed back-to-back no hitters for High Point, NC, before joining former college rival Hayes to help the Baltimore Black Sox win a 1929 pennant.

• The best players from northeastern North Carolina towns such as Weldon and Roanoke Rapids were recruited by the Louisburg team.

• By 1926 Laurinburg had a town team. New Bern fielded a ballclub that opened the 1926 campaign on April 5 at Baysboro, NC.

• Raleigh's South Park Hornets of the 1920s played most of their home games at Shaw College. Owned by a South Carolina railroad man named Will Brevard, the Hornets were managed by a man named Watkins and featured in the lineup such players as second baseman and captain Floyd "Deacon" Jones, third baseman "Jumpin'" Joe Wiggins, and standout catcher Aaron "Skink" Browning. (Browning was quite a backstop, he also played for the 1928 Wilmington, Del., Potomacs with future Hall of Fame third baseman William "Judy" Johnson.) Other players included left fielder Elijah Austin and pitcher W.A. "Pete" Wilder, who had played at Shaw College. In 1927 and 1928 they starred a fireballing pitcher named Aaron "Rabbit" Shaw. Unlike most of the others, Shaw was not a Raleigh native but he made the club in a tryout.

• The 1926 Winston-Salem White Sox, operated by Frazier W. Neal, issued, in an April 1926 edition of the *Pittsburgh Courier*, a "challenge [to] any fast team in North Carolina, Virginia, West Virginia and South Carolina." Club manager George "Red" Scales had played first base for the 1922 Pittburgh Keystones, a major eastern team.

The Asheville Royal Giants

In 1916 Asheville businessman and developer E.W. Pearson founded a baseball team called the Asheville Royal Giants. Pearson was a grocer, insurance company owner, and developer of West Asheville's Burton Street community at a time when West Asheville's black population was growing, and he always sought ways to foster prosperity and interest in the community. For years he sponsored a large agricultural fair, with carnival rides and livestock shows, that was well attended by blacks and whites; contrast that with Cleveland County, NC, where a black-only agricultural fair was founded in the 1920s. Pearson's establishment of a ball club helped fulfill his vision of West Asheville as an emerging black business hub.

Western North Carolina had very little slavery because the white farmers in the region were primarily poor, and the western part of the state was not cotton-growing country. Black population growth in Asheville can be traced primarily to three time periods, the first being the construction of the Old Buncombe Turnpike in the 1830s. The arrival of the railroad in the 1880s and the establishment of the Vanderbilt-owned Biltmore House in 1895, marked another period. (From 1887 to 1890 the black population in Asheville grew by 37 percent.) Finally, a rise in tourism due to author Thomas Wolfe's celebration of Asheville in the first two decades of the 20th century brought about even more growth.

In 1910 the West Asheville Bridge was built to connect the western section to the rest of the city, opening many employment and recreation opportunities—including baseball—to the city's black residents. Asheville's first ballpark for organized baseball, Oates Park, was built in 1914 at the triangle of Southside, Choctaw, and McDowell Streets. (Another popular ballfield at that time, Riverside Park, was destroyed by the Great Flood of July 16, 1916.) Shared by both the black and white teams of Asheville, Oates Park would become the primary home of the Royal Giants, though they also played in a park named Pearson's Park, after their owner.

White teams that played at Oates Park were members of the North

Carolina League until 1917, then the Southeastern League and the Appalachian League. In an exhibition game on April 4, 1914, rookie Jim Thorpe of the New York Giants hit a home run to help defeat Asheville. As a boy, Thomas Wolfe was a batboy for a white Asheville team that won the North Carolina League pennant in 1915. Wolfe later fashioned the character Nebraska Crane in the novel *You Can't Go Home Again* after Asheville team manager and second baseman Tom Corbett.

Though the Asheville of 1916 lived by the Jim Crow laws prevalent throughout the South, racism did not thwart black opportunity and entrepreneurship there as in some cities. Asheville's black residents enjoyed leisure time entertainment, and the Royal Giants fit the bill.

The team nickname, Royal Giants, was not uncommon for "colored" teams in the South at the time—two pre–1920 Memphis teams and a Louisville team also bore the name. These ballclubs and others adopted the name of the Brooklyn Royal Giants, who captured Eastern Colored League pennants in 1909, 1910, 1914 and 1916, the latter year marking the birth of the Asheville namesake.

Pearson's Royal Giants entertained black ballclubs from North Carolina towns and cities, from Atlanta, and from Greenville, SC (an hour's drive, and the hometown of World War One–era big leaguers "Shoeless" Joe Jackson and Red Smith). The Greenville ballclub the Royal Giants hosted was called the Greenville Black Spinners, after the Greenville Spinners of the all-white South Atlantic (or Sally) League. Only a library photograph documents a visit by the Atlanta team. The guests may have been the Atlanta Dixie Giants or the Atlanta Cubs, who were recruited from four black colleges in the summer of 1918. In 1920–21 the Cubs became the Atlanta Black Crackers, one of the Deep South's most prominent black ball clubs.

Despite some truly great talent, the level of play and organization of the southern semi-pro black teams did not, as a whole, approach that of the Negro National League to the North. Still, these clubs were the first baseball employers of the likes of John "Buck" O'Neill of Sarasota (Miami Giants) and future Hall of Famer Leroy "Satchel" Paige of Mobile, Alabama (Chattanooga Lookouts). Many black ballplayers made money with semi-pro teams as early as age 14, especially those who stopped attending secondary schools to help with family expenses. Impressive play might garner the attention of the more renowned teams in the Eastern Colored League, which began play in 1920, or the well-established Negro

Opposite: The 1916 Asheville Royal Giants. (Photograph courtesy of the North Carolina Collection, Pack Memorial Public Library, Asheville, North Carolina.)

National League. Dreams of playing in these leagues were certainly shared by members of the Asheville Royal Giants.

During the era it was customary for black ballclubs to host a festive game on Independence Day. The Royal Giants were no exception. A July 4, 1916, photograph of the Royal Giants depicts a formally dressed bleacher-seated black crowd, many of the men sporting bowlers or derbies. The dark-clad players are seated on a bench or kneeling on the grass, flanked by well-dressed citizens who were perhaps business colleagues of E.W. Pearson, community leaders, or both. Later photographs, one dated 1918, the other undefined, show 11 and 12 players respectively. The later teams sport a lighter-colored uniform emblazoned with the initials "A" for Asheville and "G" for Giants. All three photographs are handsome. A few grace the walls of Asheville establishments today.

It is noteworthy that the Royal Giants survived after Asheville's white team disbanded during the First World War. White minor league baseball did not return to the city until 1924, with the Asheville Skylanders of the Class B South Atlantic League.

Since baseball was not a full-time profession for members of the Royal Giants, many of Pearson's ballplayers worked regular jobs on trains or at Biltmore, the Vanderbilt family estate that was—and is—the largest private home in the U.S. Others were employed at historic hotels such as the Vanderbilt, the Grove Park Inn, and the Battery Park.

The last known surviving Royal Giants player was 5'8" pitcher William "Bill" Boyd, who died in Asheville in 1982. The names of many of Boyd's teammates have been forgotten over the years, but among those still recalled are such local luminaries as Mack Burton, Reverend Young, and Tom McMickens.

There is little or no existing record of the Royal Giants receiving any coverage in the printed press, though they were without a doubt one of the best professional outfits in North Carolina.

Though they were unsung on the national scene and remain but a footnote in most black baseball literature, black North Carolina teams played the best segregated competition available and launched the careers of several prominent Negro Leaguers. Early black ballplayers in the state paved the way for Tar Heel successors such as Sherman Jones (Winton, NC, starting pitcher in first Mets home game in 1962), Tom Alston (a 1940's star for Greensboro's Goshen Red Wings and the first black St. Louis Cardinal), and Tom Hall (Thomasville, NC, Cincinnati Reds).

Opposite: The 1918 Asheville Royal Giants. (Photograph courtesy of the North Carolina Collection, Pack Memorial Public Library, Asheville, North Carolina.)

Crash Davis
in His Own Words

*from interviews with Hank Utley in 1997
and Chris Holaday in 2001*

I grew up in Gastonia, North Carolina. In that town, the ultimate in life for a kid was to be on the American Legion baseball team. At the age of 11 I made one of the teams. Gastonia was set up with about six auxiliary teams, and an All-Star team was picked every year to represent Gastonia. I probably played American Legion ball longer than anyone ever played in Gastonia because they had these auxiliary teams and no Little League back then. I played shortstop, and at the age of 15 (I became 16 during the season on July 14) I finally made the All-Star team in Gastonia. That team was coached by "Doc" Newton, who was also a college coach at the time. It was a great honor to make that team.

The year I made the All-Star team was 1935. We had a great season and we went all the way to the National American Legion Championship. We beat Sacramento, California, at home in Gastonia for the title. Our town had a population of about 20,000 people at that time but one of the games in that series drew over 11,000 people. That was incredible for a town of that size.

I got my first nickname when I was playing American Legion ball. I started off being called "Little" Davis 'cause I was just a tiny thing. Later they started calling me "Squeaky" because I always had a lot of chatter, all my life. Most of our American Legion games were played in the Gastonia High School Stadium, and that was where I picked up the name "Crash." This is a true story, embellished somewhat: I was playing shortstop in a game and we had a guy by the name of Bob Russell that played left field. Somebody hit a short pop fly to left so I went back and he and I collided hard. At that time I became "Dynamite," but that exploded to "Crash" and I've been that all my life. It followed me through my school days, my professional career, right up to the movie *Bull Durham.*

I remember before I made the big team, the All-Star team in Gastonia, I was playing second and the other team had a man on third base. I went up to the pitcher and I said, 'Give me the ball' and then went back to second base. When the runner wasn't looking I was going to flip the ball

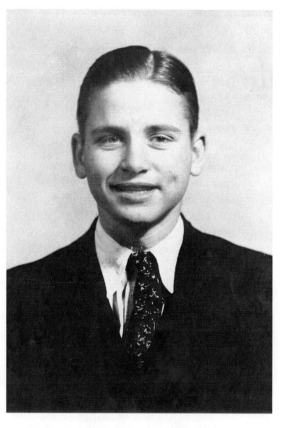

Sixteen-year-old Crash in the suit he was given for winning the National American Legion Championship. (Photograph courtesy of Crash Davis.)

to third and we would get him out. But as I was walking back to second the man scored. So they called me "Bonehead" for awhile. I had lots of names.

I think American Legion ball probably influenced my early life more than anything. One great thing I remember was we had a parade in Gastonia after we won that championship. It was a parade going down Main Street and they let us ride on the fire truck. I thought that was something. And then Warren Gardner had a clothing store and he gave each of us a suit. I had never worn a suit; that was such a thrill. That was probably the most thrilling thing that happened to me. Things like that just put you a notch ahead, and you have to take advantage of those things as they occur in life, otherwise you just don't go anywhere.

The next year, 1936, in Legion ball we got beat in the North Carolina State Finals. But that American Legion ball contributed as much to my success as anything that ever happened in my life.

A lot of kids back in those days wouldn't leave home. That '35 Legion team had a lot of talent, but they just wouldn't leave home. And some of them were a lot better ball players than I was. There's always that one opportunity you get in life, and if you don't take advantage of it you're left.

All my brothers played baseball as well when we were growing up. Hutt and I later played together in professional ball one year in the New England League. "Toad" was a catcher. He died a few years back. Bobby also played organized baseball. My Dad was a Sunday School teacher and choir director. He wouldn't let the family cheer at ball games, even though they were at all of them.

In school I always studied hard. I was a pretty good student because I did well in my books and I studied and worked hard. I loved baseball and I would be so tired when I got home. I would get up at five o'clock in the morning and study my lessons.

There was a man that took a special interest in me in Gastonia. "Boo" Boshamer was the postmaster in Gastonia, and he was quite a politician. He was a Duke graduate and he took an interest in me when I was playing American Legion ball. He was the one that carried me to Duke and introduced me to Coach Coombs. He was the one responsible for me going to Duke University.

Jack Coombs was probably the next greatest influence on my life after my father. Coaches can sometimes get into that position. Coach Coombs was kind of the type of manager Mr. Mack was. He didn't wear a baseball uniform, at least when I was there. He sat on the bench with his hat and suit. He didn't get out on the field either. Just like Mr. Mack, he always sent one of the assistant coaches out to change pitchers, and he didn't argue with the umpires. But he had a great, great knowledge of baseball. And everybody who played on his team had to take the baseball class he taught. I guess we probably learned more baseball from his class than any other source. You didn't have to be on the baseball team to take the class either.

Coach Coombs was a great teacher. He went to Colby College so he was a learned man. He was also a listener. When I had a problem I would go see Coach Jack. I really don't think he ever gave me an answer, he just let me talk it out. He was a smart man.

I remember one story that went around the school. He and his wife Miss Mary lived right there on the West Campus of Duke. They had an apartment right in the student buildings. They used to walk from their apartment across the campus to the student union for food. Miss Mary always trailed one or two steps behind Coach Coombs. One day when it was icy they were walking and Coach Coombs heard a thump behind him. He turned around and Miss Mary was lying on the ground. So he puts his hand out like an umpire and calls "safe."

Coach Coombs wrote a book about coaching. It was written during the time I was in school and they used pictures of some of us guys. My picture's in there somewhere.

We had very good teams under Coach Coombs and we won the Southern Conference. I remember that 1939 team at Duke (my sophomore year) lost only one ball game, to Maryland, up in Maryland. I was captain my senior year and I remember we didn't win the conference that year but we did my junior year.

I remember a story about that 1939 season. Back in those days we didn't have all the trainers they have now. One of our players slid into second base and hurt his ankle. So one of the guys picked up the medicine kit and rushed out to second base and opened the bag, and all that was in there was a pint of whiskey!

Every summer while I was in college I played semi-pro ball. After my freshman year I went back home to play for the Gastonia Spinners in what was called the Carolina League. They called that league an "outlaw" league because it used real professional players but it didn't follow the rules of organized professional baseball. I got more experience in that league in 1937 than any other, outside the big leagues.

Some of those ball players in the old outlaw Carolina League were tough. They were just great ball players. I was just 17 years old and I really grew up. We had a manager named Frank Packard. He was one of the toughest managers I ever played for—I mean in my whole baseball career. He was particularly tough on pitchers. He would call "time out" and then he would give pitchers holy hell. We went through so many players we had a team coming, one there, and one going. They were so anxious to win, but I made the ball club.

I had been there a week or so—I'll never forget this—there are always certain little things you remember in your career. I was struggling a little bit, but in the 8th inning of a game—I forget who it was against—I hit a high fastball over the left field fence and won the ball game. That sort of set me on fire and moved me forward. From then on I had a pretty good year. I was always a little better fielder than I was a hitter, but back in those days I could hold my own pretty good. Playing with those fellows gives you confidence. I could turn the double play as good as anyone.

That summer of 1937 I had the only fight I ever had in any league. I had a fight with a guy named George Andrews. He was a left-handed hitter, had his head shaved, and was probably in his 30s. He just didn't like college players. I don't know why. But we had a fight in the clubhouse in Concord. We had a real fight. I didn't know I could fight that well. Frank Packard got rid of him the next day.

I remember another story. It was either the first or second day I reported to Gastonia. The team had its office in the old National Bank Building. They had a club meeting, and "Alabama" Pitts, the famous ex-convict, and manager Frank Packard got into a fight. So they traded Pitts to Valdese. The next time we played in Valdese, "Alabama" got on first base and Frank covered second on a steal. "Alabama" slid head first and hit Frank right in the belly and nearly knocked him out. Frank couldn't get his breath. I was playing second and I though he was going to die. And "'Bama" was hollering, "Frank don't die, don't die or they will put me back in jail!"

I learned a lot of lessons in that league. Hickory had a big pitcher named Kermode, and in one game I hit a ball up against the fence the first time I was at bat. When I went up the second time, I sort of pointed like I was going to do it again, and Kermode hit me in the head with his first pitch. We didn't have helmets in those days and I was really hit.

For me, 1937 was an amazing year, playing against players like Bobby Hipps and with Stuffy McCrone. They were really experienced ballplayers. It was incredible. I probably learned more in that league than I did in the big leagues. I really grew up!

During the summer of '38, after my sophomore year at Duke, I played in the New England League for Rutland, Vermont. They were all college players. Jack Berry, a college coach, was our manager. I slid into second base on July 4 in Montpelier and broke my ankle, and that slowed me down a little bit. That ankle still bothers me.

In '39 I played in the Tobacco State League, another semi-pro league. I played for Sanford, North Carolina, and made $140 per month. That league included teams from towns like Zebulon and Angier, and we played about five or six games a week. They also had the state semi-pro tournament in High Point, and we went up and won that too. We really had a good ball club. Tommy Byrne and Ray Scarborough, who both went to the big leagues, they played for Wake Forest. Angier went and got them to play, and they tried to beat us but they couldn't. We didn't lose many ball games. We had three guys from Duke: myself, first baseman Eddie Shokes (he played with Cincinnati for awhile), and Glenn Price. We also had Porter Vaughan pitching for us down there. Porter played with me when I was at Philadelphia.

We drew good crowds down there. But oh, those lights. People can't imagine what it was like playing under those lights. One night I stuck a ball in my hip pocket and I told Hoover, the shortstop, to watch what happens if a ball is ever hit to my left. It was so dark out in the outfield, when a ball did go past me to my left I just took the ball out of my pocket and threw to first. They called him out! Of course, a big argument resulted from that.

Lewis Isenhour owned that team. He owned a brick company and he loved baseball. He treated us well, and boy we had fun down there. That was a great summer.

I guess that outlaw league after my freshman year is where Connie Mack noticed me because his team picked up my school tab the next year. In those days a lot of times big league teams would help pay for your college education. So in my second year at Duke, Mr. Mack and the Philadelphia Athletics did that for me. You didn't really have to sign with them, but I honored the unwritten agreement to play for them after I got out of school. I went straight from Duke to Philadelphia.

Being a southern boy I hadn't traveled too much, but when I got to Shibe Park in Philadelphia, Mr. Mack said he was going to give me $300. I said, "Mr. Mack, I won't play for that. I'm making about that much now." He said. "Well young man, if you don't want it just go home." I couldn't go home; I didn't have any money. So I signed.

But Mr. Mack was really a gentleman. I was in awe. The big leagues back then meant more than they do today—only eight teams in a league, two leagues, no television. You would read all about those guys. I was simply in awe when I saw Ted Williams, Joe DiMaggio, guys you had read about, like gods.

I didn't get in a game for about two weeks. I was sitting at the end of the bench. Mr. Mack called "Davie." He couldn't remember names very well. He said, "Davie." I said, "Yes, sir." He said, "I want you to pinch hit."

I grabbed a couple of bats, rushed up to home plate, and the umpire said, "Wait a minute son, you have to let this man hit first."

The first man I hit against was Bob Feller. To make a long story short, he was fast. But I did hit a pop fly to the catcher.

In 1941 I did really well in Spring Training but I just didn't do it after the season started. We had Spring Training in Anaheim, California. Back in those days Mr. Mack sat on the bench and moved players with his score-card. I remember he loved to sit in the lobby of hotels, since it was too hot to stay in the rooms. He liked to meet people.

I played with good ball players—Al Simmons, Wally Moses, Bob

Johnson. In 1941 Ted Williams came into Philadelphia hitting just over the .400 mark. On Saturday he went none for four and went down right on the .400 mark. He could have sat out the double header the next day and still hit .400, but he elected to play.

I played in both of those games. I played second base in the first game and first base in the second. That's a good story. We were in Chicago earlier and riding down the elevator and Mr. Mack said, "Davie, can you play first base?" I replied, "Never played it but I can." So that day I played first base against the Chicago White Sox in Comiskey Park. And this is true, too—when you play second base and a ball goes through your legs, you don't chase it. Anyway, a ball went over my head that day at first. I didn't really hustle. My cap came off and I went over to pick it up before I picked up the ball. The next day's paper said, "Davis retrieves cap before ball."

Anyway, in that final double header with the Red Sox, Porter Vaughan, who had played with me at Sanford, was one of the pitchers that pitched against Ted. People used to think that maybe we would try to throw those games, and Mr. Mack told us, "This is baseball and if I ever find out anyone is letting down I'm going to get you kicked out of baseball." But Porter was a left-handed pitcher and Ted Williams was a left-handed hitter and he'd never seen Porter. Porter was just brought up, you know. It's very difficult for a guy to hit against anybody if he's never seen them before. But it didn't stop Ted Williams, though, because he got six for eight in the double header. He's the greatest hitter who ever lived.

That was also the year DiMaggio had his 56-game hitting streak. I had a lot of experiences, but I wasn't a real good ball player in the big leagues. I made the team and got a lot of recognition, though. I remember going from Cleveland to Detroit on the boat at night. We didn't fly. We had trains. In Spring Training we worked our way back from the West Coast with the Cubs and Pirates, so I did get to hit against Dizzy Dean. He didn't have much left by then, though. Overall it was a wonderful experience for a young unmarried guy. I took it all in.

My first roommate was pitcher Chubby Dean. Chubby was a Duke guy as well, and also a North Carolina native. He was a good looking man, and on my first road trip Chubby had too many women. He wasn't married so the women were after him.

I grew up in a lot of ways in the big leagues. For a young man out of the South it was a great education. Didn't think too much about it at the time, but I wouldn't take anything for it now.

In 1942 I was drafted and I went into the Navy. My first station was in Norfolk in November of '42. I got into the physical education program.

In 1943, at the Norfolk Air Station, all I did was play baseball. We had Dom DiMaggio in center field, Pee Wee Reese at short, Eddie Robinson played first, and Hugh Casey was a pitcher. At Norfolk Naval Base just across the fence was Bob Feller and several other big leaguers. All we did was play ball.

In the fall of 1943 I was transferred to Harvard University where I became Officer of the Day in the ROTC program up there. I became a squash coach and I didn't even know what squash was. Then I moved to the Harvard baseball team. So in 1944 I helped Floyd Stahl with that team. Later I became coach of the J.V. team at Harvard. We played the prep schools around New England.

I was married in Norfolk in 1943, and my wife Harriet was with me and we lived at Harvard Square. My wife taught at Gastonia High School, and we had two daughters. We are divorced now, but we had many fruitful years together.

At Harvard I had Bobby Kennedy under me in ROTC. He wasn't a real standout. He was just an ordinary guy. He certainly didn't lead the class. He was not a battalion leader, nothing like the way he developed. Some guys get opportunities, others don't.

Like I said before, I had a lot of names—Little Davis, Squeeky, Dynamite, and then Crash. At Harvard I started playing under the name Chuck Leary in the New England Semi-Pro League. I played under an assumed name because I guess it was against the rules to play, even though it didn't hurt anything. I chose the name Leary because there are a lot of Irish in that area. In that league we played three or four games per week. We made good money, and it was extra and above my Navy money. Later I played in Woonsocket, Rhode Island. I played as Bob Palliteria—a French name since there were a lot of French people there. My wife was at one of the games, and one of the fans of French background said, "Bob Palliteria is a good ball player. Does he speak English?"

I also managed at Lawrence that same year. I remember one game when we were playing in Providence, Rhode Island, and all those players were using assumed names. Jimmy Gleeson, who had been with the Cubs and the Reds, was playing in that league, and first base was open so I elected to walk him. I didn't know that little guy that was hitting next, but I knew Gleeson. That little short guy looked about 18 or 19 years old, and it turned out he hit a home run with the bases loaded. His real name was Lawrence "Yogi" Berra. Yogi was at New London in the Merchant Marine.

After the war I was discharged in November of 1945. I returned to pro ball, but Philadelphia cut me in Spring Training. To show how cold baseball can be, they didn't even call you in and say "We're sorry you

Crash as a Raleigh Capital in the later years of his career. (Photograph courtesy of Crash Davis.)

didn't make it." They just left a pink note in your box. I needed to be a step faster. I lost that during the war. So I returned to Lawrence in 1946 and '47 to play in the Class B New England League. Don Newcombe and Roy Campanella were at Nashua in that league. I remember Roy tried to get me to go barnstorming after the '47 season down to the Caribbean. Both were great guys; Branch Rickey knew how to pick them.

I guess I was one of the first free agents in baseball. After I got released by Philadelphia I would only sign one-year contracts. I wouldn't sign unless they would give me my release at the end of the year. So after two years with Lawrence I decided to go back and do some graduate work at Duke, and I signed with the Durham Bulls for 1948.

Willie Duke was the manager in Durham. He was quite a character. Once I remember the ump made a bad decision in Durham on a Sunday afternoon and Willie took a bucket of ice water and threw it across the

plate. The ump kicked him out. Willie became one of the greatest promoters of baseball I ever knew. He started the Hot Stove League in Raleigh,
and he was responsible for me being in the North Carolina American
Legion Hall of Fame. He sponsored me. Baseball was all he lived for to
his dying day.

After a season in Durham I signed with Raleigh, which was in the
same league. I played there in '49 and had another pretty good year. In
1950 I spent part of the season with Raleigh and then went over to Rei-
dsville, another Carolina League club. For 1951 it was back to Raleigh, and
I stayed there through the '52 season. After that I decided to retire.

During the off-season when I was playing at Raleigh, I was coaching
and teaching at Bethesda High School in Durham. I coached baseball and
basketball and helped with football.

When I retired from playing I went back to Gastonia and became
baseball coach of the high school team there. We won two state champi-
onships. I also coached the American Legion team. The team I coached
in 1954, we went to the finals out in Yakima, Washington. We almost
duplicated what the 1935 Gastonia team did, but we came up a little short
against San Diego in the championship game.

Eventually I took a job with Burlington Industries. It was probably
the greatest move I ever made financially. I did personnel work with
them for 28 or 29 years. I started off in Gastonia but later transferred to
Greensboro.

I never dreamed that my baseball career would bring me any kind of
fame later in life. It was all because of that good season in Durham in 1948
when I led the league in doubles. Nearly 40 years later movie director Ron
Shelton was going through the Carolina League record book and he liked
the name Crash Davis. So that's where it all started. He used my name for
Bull Durham; he changed the doubles to home runs. I never realized that
movie was going to be so successful.

Ron Shelton and I became friends, and that's how I got in the movie
Cobb, too. He gave me a little role in that. I thought that was going to be
a real blockbuster, but there was too much psychology in it. It was kind
of depressing. They put that movie out early in the Christmas season,
thinking that with Tommy Lee Jones it was going to be an Oscar con-
tender. I wish it would have been because anytime you get a speaking part
you get residuals. But it was fun, I had a good time and Ron Shelton is a
great guy.

You know you have to be ready for changes in life. The opportunities only come once, twice, or three times and you have to take advantage
of them. It's just like I never thought I would be a celebrity of sorts in

later life because of a movie. It's like baseball, when you only get a really good pitch every so often. You know I wasn't always the best player on my team, but I always got a hit when it counted. When I think about it, that has really made all the difference in life.

Davis' professional record:

Year	Club	League	G	AB	R	H	2B	HR	RBI	AVG
1940	Philadelphia	American	23	67	4	18	1	0	9	.269
1941	Philadelphia	American	39	105	6	23	3	0	8	.219
1942	Philadelphia	American	86	272	31	61	8	2	26	.224
1946	Lawrence	New England	113	440	78	131	23	19	94	.298
1947	Lawrence/ Lowell/Pawtucket	New England	118	420	71	128	23	2	79	.300
1948	Durham	Carolina	143	540	106	171	50	10	80	.317
1949	Raleigh	Carolina	124	453	59	134	34	7	60	.296
1950	Raleigh/Reidsville	Carolina	133	497	60	130	29	4	46	.262
1951	Raleigh	Carolina	140	480	69	124	28	2	66	.258
1952	Raleigh	Carolina	116	416	55	96	15	1	41	.231

Editor's note: Lawrence "Crash" Davis passed away on August 31, 2001, at the age of 82.

The All-Time
North Carolina Team

by Matthew Eddy

The first few names spring to mind easily: Luke Appling, Catfish Hunter, Gaylord Perry. All three North Carolinians by birth. But were one to construct an all-time all–North Carolina team, which players would fill out the 25-man roster?

I have taken up the necessary task of compiling such a team, in which only players born outside the state boundaries of North Carolina are disqualified. To prevent the exploitation of one position's wealth, and to give the process a modern feel, the roster was created as if the team would be taking the field in the year 2002. That is, roster slots are assigned as follows: five starting pitchers, five relief pitchers, two catchers, eight infielders and five outfielders.

Seven Hall of Famers hail from North Carolina. Three of them— Hunter, Perry and Hoyt Wilhelm—were fantastic pitchers, two of them pitching effectively into their forties. Just don't expect the trend of great pitchers being in the minority to hold.

Matthew Eddy hails from central New York state and is currently employed by Baseball America in Durham, North Carolina. A 2000 graduate of St. Bonaventure University, he devotes more energy to following the Mets than is recommended by the Surgeon General for emotional well being.

Simply put, the state of North Carolina has contributed vastly more quality pitchers than quality hitters to the big leagues. All told, however, the team is quite balanced. (Of course I'd say that; I selected the team.) But you shall see that soon enough. With apologies to Razor Shines, Harvey Grubb and George Suggs, then, I present to you Team North Carolina, beginning with the starting pitching staff.

Top to bottom, the rotation is solid and, with the inclusion of the left-handed Lanier, somewhat balanced.

Pitcher

Gaylord Perry (b. 9/15/38 Williamston), the staff ace, gained notoriety for his mastery and repeated use of the "super-slider," a pitch that resembled a spitball in every way but one: Umpires were unsuccessful in preventing Perry from throwing the prohibited pitch. Perry was so elusive in his chicanery that he thrived even after the rules forbade a pitcher from going to his mouth. Armed with a wide array of lubricants and other creams—Vaseline, KY Jelly, Preparation H—the right-hander doctored the baseball for 22 big league seasons, or long enough for him to amass 314 victories.

While his won-lost percentage, .542, is the lowest of the starting five, Perry has a valid excuse: he played for some lousy teams after he was traded from the Giants following the 1971 season. Consider this: for his ten years in San Francisco, his Giants teams posted a .563 winning percentage. His remaining 12 seasons saw his teams post a .470 mark. It's hard to win games as a starting pitcher when the club itself doesn't often win.

Amid all the losing seasons, though, he emerged with two Cy Young awards, one in each league. This was, of course, before the days of Pedro Martinez and Randy Johnson, making him the first (and for 21 years the only) pitcher to accomplish the feat. With Cleveland in 1972, his first season in the American League, Perry went 24–16 with a 1.92 ERA and led the league with 29(!) complete games. After five years on the Junior Circuit, Perry made his way back to the National League in 1978. This time a Padre, he greeted opposing batters with a 21–6 record and a 2.73 ERA, while leading the league with his .778 winning percentage.

Gaylord Perry entered the Hall of Fame in 1991, with a great strikeout-to-walk ratio of 2.6. For his career, he whiffed 3,534 batters against 1,379 walks. Opposing batters managed a .245 batting average off him for his career.

A five-time World Series winner with the 1970s' two dynasties other than the Big Red Machine, **Catfish Hunter** (b. 4/8/46 Hertford) retired at the age of 33 with 224 victories. Had he pitched until he was 40 he may have won 300 games. Clearly, he wasn't driven by statistical goals, opting instead to return to North Carolina to do the things he did before becoming a ballplayer.

If not the ace of great Athletics squads of the early '70s and the Yankees teams late in the decade, Hunter was certainly a key contributor. Of the six World Series he participated in (1972–74 with A's, 1976–78 with Yankees), he landed zero Game One starts. Ken Holtzman, Doyle Alexander, Don Gullett and Tommy John were awarded those assignments. In his defense, Hunter's squads appeared in seven American League Championship Series, in which he started three ('72, '74, '76) Game Ones. (Note that he was not on the Yankees' 1977 ALCS roster.)

A 1987 electee to the Hall of Fame, Hunter took home the AL Cy Young award in his final season with the A's (1974) with one of his finest performances. His 2.49 ERA paced the league and his 25 wins were also tops. That season is nearly indistinguishable from the four before it and the one after it. During Hunter's incredible five-year run from 1971 to 1975 he never won fewer than 21 games, and his ERA ranged from 2.04 to 3.34. He slipped rather markedly after the '76 season, however, as he would never start more than 22 games or throw more than 105 innings in a season for the balance of his record-breaking five-year, $3.75 million pact with New York. Never an overpowering pitcher, he struck out 2,012 batters in his 3,449⅓ big league innings. Clearly the key to his success was control—he walked just 954 and surrendered a career .231 opponents' batting average.

Wes Ferrell (b. 2/2/08 Greensboro) won 20 games in each of his first four seasons. He accomplished the feat twice more before he retired from major league baseball at age 33.

The temperamental right-hander relied on a terrific fastball during his early years (though his walks outnumbered his strikeouts twice in the aforementioned four-year span), but when his fastball abandoned him in 1933, so did his club. The Indians traded Ferrell to the Red Sox the next year, where he was united with his kid brother, catcher Rick Ferrell. The two had a contentious relationship while battery mates, with Wes allegedly shaking off Rick's signs to draw his ire and demonstrate his disrespect for Rick's game-calling skills. The honeymoon lasted until 1937 when both brothers were traded—wonder of wonders—to the Senators. Rick played on in the nation's capital until 1941; Wes was traded the next season.

A case could be made for Wes Ferrell's enshrinement, but it's hard to ignore a 4.04 ERA (even in the context of the high scoring '30s), which would be the highest of any Hall pitcher. The writers agreed, as Ferrell garnered one vote each of the first two years of eligibility (1956–57), while peaking at eight votes in 1960, two years before his removal from the ballot.

Of course, Ferrell's claim to immortality wasn't really his right arm but his bat. Arguably the best hitting pitcher of all time, Ferrell conked 38 home runs—or ten more than his brother, and the most by any pitcher—and batted .280 for his career. His slugging average, too, was higher than Rick's—.446 to .363—albeit in 4,852 fewer at-bats.

As an outfielder in the minor leagues following his big league pitching career, Wes Ferrell won the Western Carolina League batting title with an amazing .425 average in 1948.

Overshadowed by his younger brother Gaylord, **Jim Perry** (b. 10/30/35 Williamston) nonetheless carved out a productive 17-season big league career. In fact, Bill James notes in his *Historical Baseball Abstract* that on September 22, 1975, the Perry brothers had identical 215–174 marks. They would ultimately finish second on the all-time brothers wins list behind Joe and Phil Niekro, but not by much. The Perry brothers amassed 529 wins compared to the Niekros' 539, but the former duo had a much better winning percentage, .546 to .530.

Jim Perry spent his best years with the Minnesota Twins from 1963 to 1972, sandwiched between appearances with Cleveland and brief stints with the Tigers and A's. He captured the American League's top pitcher award in 1970, beating Baltimore's Dave McNally by eight votes for the Cy Young award. In that fateful 1970 season, Perry went 24–12 with a 3.04 ERA. He also notched a career-high strikeout mark of 168.

Perry saw limited action as a reliever in the Twins' first World Series appearance in 1965, which they lost four games to three to the Dodgers. Four years later he was the ace of the Carew-Killebrew-Oliva Twins teams that were swept in the '69 and '70 ALCS, each time by the Orioles.

Rounding out the all–North Carolina five-man rotation is southpaw **Max Lanier** (b. 8/18/15 Denton). Lanier spent all but two of his 14 big-league seasons with the Cardinals. (He spent his final seasons with the Giants and Browns.) Used as both a starter and reliever throughout his career (327 games, 204 starts), he started four World Series games for the Cards from 1942 to 1944, going a combined 2–1 for the stretch. (He did-n't participate in the 1946 series; he had just six starts on the year but was 6–0.)

Lanier enjoyed his best season in 1943 when he compiled a 15–7 record and a 1.90 ERA in 32 appearances, 25 of them starts. Referenced in Philip Roth's fictitious tale of baseball and Communist conspiracy, *The Great American Novel,* Lanier's most famous start was the sixth and deciding game of the '44 Series. In it he surrendered just one run to the crosstown Browns in five innings of work to record the victory. He compiled a 1.73 ERA in World Series play over 31 2⁄3 innings of work.

Blessed with two of the best starters of the last fifty years in Hunter and Gaylord Perry, North Carolina was also home to **Hoyt Wilhelm** (b. 7/26/23 Huntersville), arguably baseball's best relief pitcher. He held the record for appearances with 1,070 until being surpassed in recent years by Dennis Eckersley and Jesse Orosco. His 123 relief wins remains a record.

A study of unusual and ironic firsts, Wilhelm first reached the big leagues at age 28, but he made up for it by pitching until he was 48 on the strength of his knuckleball. In 1958 the Orioles expanded his role for the first time from exclusive relief pitcher to occasional starter. He notched a no-hitter in one of only four starts with the Orioles—against the World Series–winning Yankees no less. He appeared in 39 games that year. Wilhelm also hit a home run in his first big league at-bat. He would never hit another, and he sported just a .088 lifetime average.

Before ever throwing a pitch (it probably would have been a knuckleball) in the majors, Wilhelm was injured in World War II at the Battle of the Bulge. He was awarded the Purple Heart.

Just once in his 22-season career did Wilhelm participate in the postseason, when his 1954 New York Giants won the World Series. His tenure with the Cardinals, Indians, Orioles, White Sox, Braves, Cubs and Dodgers resulted in zero playoff appearances.

Wilhelm enjoyed his best overall performance in 1964 for the White Sox when he posted a 1.99 ERA and went 12–9 in 73 games, pitching 131⅓ innings. Additionally, he paced the American League with a 2.19 ERA in 1959 as an Oriole; and in his rookie season with the Giants he led the National League in ERA (2.43), games (71) and winning percentage (.833).

By today's inflated save standards, Wilhelm's total of 227 seems insignificant. Bearing in mind how relief pitcher usage patterns have changed since the fifties and sixties, the balance achieved by Wilhelm in relief wins and saves is remarkable. It took awhile to get there, but Wilhelm was finally elected to the Hall of Fame in 1985 in his eighth year of eligibility.

Tom Zachary (b. 5/7/1896 Graham) pitched for 19 seasons, mostly as a starting pitcher with seven big league clubs—the Athletics, Senators, Browns, Yankees, Braves, Dodgers and Phillies. His 125 relief appearances, though, constitute nearly one-quarter of his 533 career appearances. And by virtue of being a left-hander, he's an easy choice for a bullpen spot.

One gets the feeling, however, that like most left-handed specialists Zachary would retain his title solely on his handedness. He worked 3,126⅓ big-league innings, and in those innings he allowed 3,580 hits, while walking 914 and striking out 720. But he kept the ball in the park: He surrendered just 119 home runs, the most famous of which was Babe Ruth's 60th in 1927. Maybe Steve Trachsel will be that famous some day for serving up Mark McGwire's 62nd.

On the plus side, his 3.73 ERA is respectable for the era in which he pitched, and he was a key component of two of the Senators' three-ever pennant-winners in 1924 and '25. He also won a World Series game with the Yankees in 1928 on their way to sweeping the Cardinals.

Zachary's 1924 season—the year of the Senators' only World Series triumph—was his finest. He posted a 2.47 ERA to complement his 15 victories. When all was said and done, Tom Zachary received two votes for the Hall of Fame, one in 1958 and the other in 1960.

A veteran of 13 seasons, **Johnny Allen** (b. 9/30/05 Lenoir) twice led the American League in winning percentage. His 17–4 record in his rookie season (1932) with the Yankees resulted in a .810 mark; similarly, his 15–1 record with the Indians in 1937 gave him an unsurpassed (on the season) .938 winning percentage. Allen was at his best in 1936 when he won 20 games for the only time in his career, while posting a 3.44 ERA and a personal-best 165 strikeouts.

Versatility would make Allen a valuable member of Team North Carolina. The right-hander made 241 starts and 111 relief appearances for his career, which included appearances in the 1932 and 1941 World Series with the Yankees and Dodgers, respectively. One vote in the 1955 Hall of Fame balloting separates Allen from the other faceless quality pitchers of years gone by.

Ted Abernathy (b. 3/6/33 Stanley) worked predominately as a relief pitcher throughout his 14-year career, twice leading his league in saves and three times in games pitched. For his career, he logged only 34 starts among his 681 appearances, giving our team its second full-time reliever.

Playing for the Senators, Indians, Cubs, Braves, Reds, Cardinals and Royals, Abernathy never sniffed the postseason. He was, however, deemed the most valuable pitcher for the 1967 season by *Total Baseball*, as measured by their total pitcher index. His 4.5 TPI in '67 edged Jim Bunning's mark by four-tenths of a point. The Reds' ace reliever recorded a career-low 1.27 ERA that season to accompany his league-leading 28 saves and 70 games pitched.

Abernathy first led the league in saves with 31 as a Cub in 1965. Though the National League didn't begin recording saves as an official statistic until 1969, *The Sporting News* started tracking save figures in 1960.

The fifth and final bullpen spot shall be awarded to left-hander **Cliff Melton** (b. 1/3/12 Brevard), whose accomplishments I consider more valuable than those of finalist Lee Meadows (b. 7/12/1894 Oxford), the first player to wear glasses on the field. The choice is a tough one, though, made more difficult by the fact that Meadows played seven more seasons than Melton and posted a better ERA, however slight the margin.

Melton is not the clear winner, in my mind, solely because he is left-handed. (It's because he was nicknamed "Mountain Music.") An investigation of his statistical performance reveals him to be an average big league pitcher after turning in his stellar rookie season. But what a season it was.

Playing his entire eight-year career for the Giants, Melton broke into the league in 1937 by winning 20 games, losing just nine and posting a 2.61 ERA. He also struck out 142 batters, more than he ever would again. Early in the '40s, Melton developed bone chips in his elbow that would cut short his career. The '37 season represents Melton's high-water mark, but compare it to Meadows' best effort. Take your pick of either his 1926 season (20–9, 3.97, 54 strikeouts) with the Pirates or his 1923 season (17–13, 3.83, 76 strikeouts) split between the Phillies and Pirates.

Neither pitcher performed well in World Series play. Melton got shelled in two starts in the '37 Series (as a rookie, mind you) in a four-games-to-one drubbing by the Yankees. He went 0–2 with a 4.91 ERA in his two starts and one relief appearance. Not even Carl Hubbell could bail him out.

Meadows, meanwhile, was 0–2 with a 6.38 ERA in two Series starts for the Pirates, one in a winning effort over the Senators in 1925, the other in a losing effort to the '27 Yankees.

On the merits of his peak performance, then, Cliff Melton is in, and Lee Meadows is out.

Turning to offense, Team North Carolina boasts a group of hitters with good to great defensive attributes and solid on-base skills. What they don't have is power.

Catcher

Though **Rick Ferrell** (b. 10/12/05 Durham) played third fiddle to the American League's two premier catchers of the thirties—Mickey Cochrane and Bill Dickey—the Veteran's Committee recognized him as a Hall of Famer nonetheless in 1984.

Ferrell caught the entire nine innings for the American League in the very first All-Star Game in 1933. In another show of durability, Ferrell for 41 years held the AL record of 1,805 games caught until Carlton Fisk broke it in 1988.

A tribute to his defensive prowess, the backstop caught for a starting pitching staff that included four knuckleballers in 1945 while a member of the Senators. It was in Washington, too, that Rick was paired for the second time with his brother Wes, a pitcher. They had previously spent part or all of the 1934–37 seasons as Red Sox teammates. (For more on the exploits of Rick and Wes, read the Wes Ferrell entry in the starting pitcher section.)

Ferrell was at his best offensively in 1936. Playing for the Red Sox, he hit .312 and posted career highs in home runs (eight), on-base percentage (.406) and slugging percentage (.461).

In direct contrast to Ferrell, **Smoky Burgess** (b. 2/6/27 Caroleen) batted left, excelled at the plate and offered only average defensive skills. *Total Baseball* pegs him with minus 96 fielding runs, by definition meaning his work behind the plate cost his teams 96 runs over the course of his 18-year career. Whatever you decide to make of that metric, it's safe to say Burgess did not play gold glove–caliber defense. But with the fourth-highest slugging mark on the team he can't be denied.

A six-time all-star, Burgess was renowned as a pinch-hitter and batted as high as .368 in a season, with as many as 28 home runs, even though as a catcher he never batted more than 442 times in any season. As the starting catcher for the '60 Pittsburgh Pirates, he hit .333 in 18 World Series at-bats, but he enjoyed his best regular-season performance six years earlier. Burgess, in 1954 with the Phillies, hit .368 with 27 homers and career-best on-base and slugging marks of .437 and .510.

First Base

Mark Grace (b. 6/28/64 Winston-Salem) has carved out his niche as one of the better first basemen of his generation. He's never been considered the best at his position in his league and he'll probably never see Cooperstown, but of the skills he possesses—the ability to get on base, hit for average and hit doubles—Grace excels. And given the dearth of hard-hitting first sackers born in North Carolina, Grace is an easy choice for the team.

As the Cubs' sure-handed first baseman for 13 years, Grace was rewarded with four ('92, '93, '95, '96) Gold Gloves, before J.T. Snow brought his sparkling defensive reputation to the National League.

The current Arizona Diamondbacks' first baseman enjoyed his best season in 1995 when he paced the league with 51 doubles and hit .326 with 16 homers, 92 runs batted in and 97 runs scored. That same season he established a career-high .516 slugging percentage and posted a Grace-like .395 on-base percentage. All this in 143 games.

Though he'll probably leave the game as one of the forgotten good players, Grace will always hold the distinction of having collected the most hits (1,754) and doubles (364) of the 1990s.

Hall of Fame Negro League first baseman **Walter "Buck" Leonard** (b. 9/8/07 Rocky Mount), nicknamed "the black Gehrig," was a key contributor to the Homestead Grays' run of dominance in the 1930s and '40s. Teaming with legendary slugger Josh Gibson, "the black Babe Ruth," the Grays took home the Negro National League pennant in nine consecutive seasons. Leonard was elected to the Hall of Fame in 1972.

Negro League statistics that do exist are highly susceptible to error due to poor or nonexistent record keeping. Furthermore, no way to properly measure the talent level of Leonard's competition exists, nor does a way to determine how ballpark factors aided or handicapped him. As such, I can't in good faith name Leonard the starter, despite anecdotal evidence that he was superior to Grace (and almost the entire Negro National League) as a hitter and as a fielder. These selections are, after all, based primarily on documented statistical accomplishment.

The best estimates by *Total Baseball* credit Leonard with a lifetime .336 average. As for home run output, this is what James A. Riley's *The Biographical Encyclopedia of the Negro League Baseball Leagues* has to say: "Following the 1943 season Leonard was credited with averaging 34 home runs per year for the past eight years." I'll leave that open to your interpretation.

Second Base

Like the catchers on the all–Carolina team, the two finest second basemen from the Tarheel State represent statistical opposites. **Billy Goodman** (b. 3/22/26 Concord) is all-hit, no-field; while **Pep Young** (b. 8/29/07 Jamestown) was renowned for his fielding.

Good defense comes with the territory at second base, so examination of the two players' glovework is in order. Young is credited with 17 fielding runs by *Total Baseball* for his career, of which 532 of his 730 games were logged at second. Goodman, meanwhile, collected minus 63 fielding runs, but in his case just 624 of his 1,623 games were played at second base, his primary position. Ironically, he led the American League in fielding runs once with 20 in 1952 while taking on the unenviable task of replacing Bobby Doerr in Boston. (Note that the metric fielding runs is not an end-all measure of a player's defensive worth; however, a highly negative number, like Goodman's, or a highly positive number, like Hal Lanier's below, can safely be labeled indicative of a player's general defensive worth.)

With Pittsburgh in 1938, Pep Young, too, paced his league in fielding runs with 32.

Offensively, the differences are just as stark. Goodman led the AL in batting with a .354 mark in 1950 with the Sox, the same season he recorded his highest on-base (.427) and slugging (.455) marks. For his first ten seasons in the league, Goodman walked at least twice as many times as he struck out.

Young's offensive explosion occurred in 1938 when he batted .278, with .329 and .381 marks for his on-base and slugging percentages.

Beginning in 1935, Young kept his starting job in Pittsburgh for just four seasons. Goodman latched on with the other Sox in 1958 and played with regularity that season and the next as a member of the "Go-Go Sox." He stuck around long enough to finish with the 1962 infant Houston Colt .45s.

Shortstop

Luke Appling (b. 4/2/07 High Point) entered baseball's Hall of Fame in 1964 as perhaps the best shortstop the game had ever seen, save Honus Wagner, and the best all-around player from North Carolina. A seven-time all-star, Appling sparked the White Sox lineup—primarily as its leadoff hitter—for twenty seasons (1930–50; he spent 1944 playing for Uncle Sam), finishing with a career .310 average and a .399 on-base percentage. Established as the club's everyday shortstop in 1932, Appling reached base only 32.9 percent of the time. On his way to becoming a prototypical leadoff hitter, that mark rose to .379 the next year, peaked at .474 three years after that and never slipped below .342 until his swan song 1950 season in which he participated in only 50 games.

Aptly nicknamed "Old Aches and Pains" for his famous and frequent hypochondriac lapses, Appling in 1943 simultaneously paced the American League with an on-base percentage of .419 and a .328 batting average.

His league-leading .388 average in 1936 was the highest such mark posted by a shortstop in the 20th century.

Never a power hitter, Appling managed only 45 career home runs and just a .398 slugging average. He nonetheless finished his career with 1,116 runs batted in, to go with his 1,319 runs scored. Contributing to his stellar on-base percentage were his other two noteworthy offensive feats: A career 2.5 walk-to-strikeout ratio (1,302 walks, 528 strikeouts) and a collection of 2,749 base hits.

Among his defensive accomplishments at shortstop, Appling is fifth all-time in games logged, seventh in putouts, fifth in assists, and fourth in double plays. He also led the league in errors six times, and his defense is popularly said to have gone from bad to acceptable.

Unlike Chicago's other Hall of Fame shortstop, Luis Aparicio (of '59 "Go-Go Sox" fame), Appling never participated in postseason play. In fact, the White Sox teams he played for finished in the second division in all but six of his seasons. Times were tough on Chicago's south side: The Chi-Sox' best showings of the Appling era were three third-place finishes and three fourth-place finishes. While the Yankees certainly made winning difficult for other AL clubs of the thirties and forties, Appling's teams compiled a meek 1,374–1,672 record, good for a .451 winning percentage. The club was an aggregate 606.5 games out of first place. For comparison, Aparicio's ten Sox teams (1956–62, 1968–70) were a combined 800–780, or .506, with one pennant and two second-place finishes.

Also of interest is how narrowly statistical analysis separates Luke Appling from his contemporary and fellow Hall of Famer Joe Cronin. Cronin was immortalized in 1956, eight years before Appling. In his *Historical Baseball Abstract*, Bill James assigns Cronin a .631 offensive winning percentage. Appling receives a .635 mark. The best efforts of *Total Baseball*, meanwhile, bestow Appling with a 40.7 total player ranking. Cronin is right behind him at 39.4.

A team featuring Luke Appling as its starter doesn't have much need for a backup shortstop. And given the lack of quality shortstops born in North Carolina, that's a good thing. **Hal Lanier** (b. 7/4/42 Denton) qualifies as next best. Absolutely anemic with the bat, Lanier more than made up for it with his defense. *Total Baseball*'s attempt at qualifying defense justifies his existence as a big league shortstop, despite not having a cool nickname like Appling.

Lanier is credited with contributing 132 fielding runs over his ten-year career, the 61st best figure of all time—among players at every position. This translates into 14.1 fielding wins, exactly 50th on the all time list. (Appling, for the record, does not crack the top 100 for either list.)

Before moving to shortstop in 1967, where he spent four years as a starter, Lanier was the Giants' starting second baseman from his rookie 1964 season through 1966. Lanier has ties to two other all–North Carolina team members. His father, Max, is a starter for the team, and Hal played alongside third baseman Jim Ray Hart with the Giants for eight years. The two again played together for the Yankees in 1973, Lanier's last year in the big leagues. Additionally, Lanier garnered one Hall of Fame vote in 1979, and he would go on to manage the Astros to the NLCS in 1986. He compiled a 254–232 mark in three years with Houston.

Third Base

Jim Ray Hart (b. 10/30/41 Hookerton) brings the thunder. As the leader in both home runs and slugging percentage among Team North Carolinians, Hart is its undisputed cleanup hitter—but also one of its worst fielders.

Hart got off to a quick start to his career, establishing himself as a legitimate power threat, before hitting the wall in 1969, losing his starting job and being relegated to the outfield. Hart connected for 31 home runs as a rookie in 1964 and collected 81 runs batted in. His power output remained strong for the next four years, with 23 home runs and 96 RBIs the next year, and 33–93, 29–99 and 23–78 the three years following. That was all the Giants ever got out of Hart, and he was picked up by the Yankees in '73, where he played his best position, designated hitter, for a few years before retiring.

Like Burgess and Goodman, Hart had his troubles afield. He accumulated minus 73 fielding runs (*Total Baseball*) over his career. It's difficult to even conceive of a player costing his team 73 runs with his defensive liabilities, but with Hart's switch to full-time outfielder in '69 it's clear the Giants had some understanding of this.

Buddy Lewis (b. 8/10/16 Gastonia), a lifelong Senator, was twice named to the American League all-star team. And like Hart, Lewis split his time between third and the outfield. But, unlike Hart, Lewis prevented runs with his defense—eleven of them, in fact, by *Total Baseball*'s count.

Lewis turned in his best season in 1939 when he led the AL in triples with 16, while hitting .319. He also slugged a career-best .478, while reaching base almost exactly 40 percent of the time. Four times Lewis hit over .300, and not once did he accumulate more strikeouts than walks in a full season.

Outfield

Enos Slaughter (b. 4/27/16 Roxboro) embodied the scrappy, hustling ballplayer better than perhaps anyone of his era. And he was a pretty darn good player, too.

"Country" spent his first 13 campaigns in St. Louis as the team's right fielder, where he contributed to two World Series victories for the Redbirds and led the NL in scattered categories throughout his career. In 1942 (Stan Musial's rookie season) the upstart Cardinals dethroned the mighty Joe DiMaggio–led Yankees in five games. That year Slaughter enjoyed perhaps his finest season. He paced the league in hits with 188, and triples with 17, as well as batting .318, slugging .494 and reaching base at a .412 rate. In that season's World Series he smacked a game-tying home run in the fifth and deciding game.

Due to his service in the U.S. military, Slaughter would not see time in a big-league outfield again until 1946. In his absence, the Cardinals would advance to the Series twice more, winning once and losing once. Upon his return in '46, he promptly led the National League with 130 runs batted in and helped guide the Cardinals to another title.

His performance in that year's Series is legendary, based almost entirely on his Mad Dash. With the score tied at three in the eighth inning of game seven versus the Red Sox, Slaughter singled to lead off the frame. But two outs later he remained at first base. Harry Walker, the fourth batter of the eighth, then lined the ball over the shortstop's head, prompting a frenzied Slaughter (with a broken elbow no less) to scamper the remaining 270 feet to the plate. He beat the relay throw, and Cardinal reliever Harry Brecheen made the run stand up in the Boston ninth.

Slaughter was named to the 1946 NL all-star team and didn't miss another one until 1954, his first year in the AL with the Yankees. Though Slaughter played until he was 43, the latter years of his career were hampered by chronic injuries. Notorious for playing in pain, the proud outfielder never let on that he was ailing.

His playing time diminished greatly with the switch in leagues, though he did play on three pennant-winning Yankees clubs (1956–58). For his final six seasons he batted just .272 (compared with .305 before the league switch).

Slaughter was immortalized with his induction into the Hall of Fame as a Veteran's Committee selection in 1985.

Charley Jones (b. 4/30/1850 Alamance County) patrolled the outfield so long ago that his career's start predates even the National League's formation by a year. Jones played sparingly in his first professional season,

1875, amassing just 51 at-bats for the National Association's Hartford and Western clubs.

The next year he joined the Cincinnati Red Stockings of the infant National League and saw action in all but one game for the cellar-dwelling (9–56) club. He batted .286 that season. Jones came into his own the following year, finishing second in slugging (.471), triples (10) and walks (15).

As a member of the Boston Nationals in 1879, Jones had unquestionably his best season. In addition to leading the circuit in runs (85), home runs (9), runs batted in (62) and walks (29), he helped the Nationals finish second in the eight-team league.

Jones enjoyed one more productive season with Boston in 1880 before jumping to the fledgling American Association to start the 1883 season. With no context in which to judge what baseball was like in the 1880s American Association (or the 1880s NL for that matter), it's difficult to gauge how good Jones really was. He led the league in on-base percentage (.376) in 1884, sure, but how competitive was a 14-league team still in its formative years? I'll give the benefit of the doubt, however, to the man who hit 56 home runs and slugged .443 in 11 dead-ball seasons.

Team North Carolina's third starting outfielder, **Taffy Wright** (b. 8/10/11 Tabor City), was a nondescript starting major league outfielder for seven seasons with the Senators and White Sox. He played in nine seasons but missed three prime years to World War II.

Though he batted. 311 for his career, Wright never led the American League in any category. Nor did he play on a playoff team. Wright's claim to fame is his 13-game streak of collecting at least one RBI per contest, the AL record he set in 1941. Taffy Wright, at his best that year, drove in 97 runs, smashed 35 doubles, hit .322, reached base at a .399 clip and slugged .468.

Wes Covington (b. 3/27/32 Laurinburg) displayed exceptional power as a part-time outfielder for the Milwaukee Braves in their pennant-winning 1957 and '58 seasons. In '57, his second season, Covington hit 21 home runs in 328 at-bats, with a slugging average of .537. The next year he produced similar results: 24 homers in 294 at-bats, with a phenomenal .622 slugging mark. That would be as good as it would ever get for Covington.

Always a liability afield, Covington lost his stroke in the 1959 season when his home run ratio plummeted (seven in 373 at-bats) and he couldn't consistently reach base (.331 on-base percentage). He had three more seasons similar to that one before turning out another good year.

In 1963, then with the Phillies, Covington hit .303, with 17 home runs and 64 RBI in 353 at-bats, and his .521 slugging percentage cleared .500 for the first time since the '58 season.

In all, Covington played 11 seasons and retired from baseball with 131 homers and a .466 slugging percentage, both figures very respectable for the low offensive era in which he played.

Trot Nixon (b. 4/11/74 Durham) seems like an unlikely choice for All-Carolina Team honors, but given the scarcity of good outfielders born in the state, the Red Sox' right fielder gets the nod.

While he still hasn't turned in the one dominating season everyone expected when he was drafted, Nixon is, in reality, one of the better right fielders in the American League. In addition to being an excellent defender, at age 27 he has hit .277, slugged .479 and posted a respectable .367 on-base average. Not bad for a guy who started playing every day (except versus lefties) only three years ago. And the memory of his game-winning home run against Roger Clemens to down the Yankees in May of 2000 will live on.

Nixon's selection has been made, of course, with an eye toward the future. He has a ways to go to match the accomplishments of Enos Slaughter, but I can think of no reason for him not to be able to establish himself as a big leaguer on equal footing with Covington, Jones or Wright.

Pitching Staff

Starters	Won-Lost	Pct.	ERA	Seasons	Years Active
Gaylord Perry, rhp	314–265	.542	3.11	22	1962–83
Jim "Catfish" Hunter, rhp	224–166	.574	3.26	15	1965–79
Wes Ferrell, rhp	193–128	.601	4.04	15	1927–41
Jim Perry, rhp	215–174	.553	3.45	17	1959–75
Max Lanier, lhp	108–8	.568	3.01	14	1938–53

Relievers	Won-Lost	Saves	ERA	Seasons	Years Active
Hoyt Wilhelm, rhp	143–122	227	2.52	21	1952–72
Tom Zachary, lhp	186–191	22	3.73	19	1918–36
Johnny Allen, rhp	142–75	18	3.75	13	1932–44
Ted Abernathy, rhp	63–69	148	3.46	14	1955–72
Cliff Melton, lhp	86–80	16	3.42	8	1937–44
*Lee Meadows, rhp	188–180	7	3.37	15	1915–29

*Honorable mention

Position players

Lineup	Bats	Avg.	OBP	SLG	HR	Seasons	Years Active
Luke Appling, ss	R	.310	.399	.398	45	20	1930–50
Mark Grace, 1b	L	.307	.386	.447	163	14	1989–present
Enos Slaughter, rf	L	.300	.382	.453	169	19	1938–59
Jim Ray Hart, 3b	R	.278	.348	.467	170	12	1963–74
Charley Jones, cf	R	.299	.347	.443	56	11	1875–88
Taffy Wright, lf	L	.311	.376	.423	38	9	1938–49
Rick Ferrell, c	R	.281	.378	.363	28	18	1929–47
Billy Goodman, 2b	L	.300	.377	.378	19	16	1947–62

Bench	Bats	Avg.	OBP	SLG	HR	Seasons	Years Active
Smoky Burgess, c	L	.295	.364	.446	126	18	1949–67
Buck Leonard, 1b	L	—	—	—	—	—	1933–50
Pep Young, 2b	R	.262	.308	.380	32	10	1933–45
Buddy Lewis, 3b	L	.297	.368	.420	71	11	1935–49
Hal Lanier, ss	R	.228	.256	.275	8	10	1964–73
Wes Covington, of	L	.279	.339	.466	131	11	1956–66
Trot Nixon, of	L	.277	.367	.479	54	5	1996–present

The All-Time
South Carolina Team

by Matthew Eddy

In sharp contrast to their North Carolinian brethren, an all-time team comprised of South Carolina's finest players would feature an abundance of offense and a thin pitching staff.

Despite boasting just one Hall of Famer (Larry Doby), Team South Carolina's power-hitting lineup probably would not struggle to score runs, at least via the home run. The 15 position players who comprise the team's offense batted an aggregate .283, with 1,613 home runs and 9,339 runs batted in. That works out to roughly 108 homers and nearly 623 RBI per player over the course of his career. For comparison, the North Carolina team had a higher batting average at .292 but had a significantly lower home run total of 1,068. Excluding Buck Leonard's contributions (his Negro League stats are incomplete and potentially inaccurate), the North Carolinian squad averaged 76 homers per man over the course of his career. It should be noted, though, that their RBI total, 8,933, while lower overall, produces an average of 638 per player for his career, or 15 more than the South Carolinians managed.

With team selection guidelines firmly entrenched in the reader's mind from the previous piece, let's examine each of Team South Carolina's position players.

Catcher

Aaron Robinson (b. 6/23/15 Lancaster) carved out a career for himself as a receiver with good on-base skills and moderate power. None of Robinson's seasons can be mistaken for those of the all-time great catchers, but what he did in 1946 with the Yankees merits recognition as his best performance. That year Robinson batted .297 in 330 at-bats, with a .388 on-base percentage and a career-high 16 home runs and .506 slugging percentage.

Playing for the Yankees in '47, Robinson made both his sole All-Star Game appearance and his sole World Series appearance. In the latter he batted .200 while playing three of the Series' seven games against Brooklyn. He also drove in one run and scored two in the Yankees' victorious effort.

For his career, Robinson posted a stellar .375 on-base percentage, with 337 walks against just 194 strikeouts.

Mickey Livingston (b. 11/15/14 Newberry), a contemporary of Robinson, enjoyed a lengthier career (10 seasons to eight) than did Robinson, but not the statistical achievement. Playing for the Senators, Phillies, Cubs, Giants, Braves and Dodgers, Livingston was not exactly a feared hitter, as he batted just .238 for his career, with puny on-base and slugging percentages of .301 and .326.

As the starting catcher for the Cubs' last pennant-winning team (1945), Livingston excelled in the World Series, batting .364 in six games, while driving in four runs and scoring three others. He didn't homer.

First Base

Though South Carolina's collection of players is generally strong offensively, first base suffers a bit from the lack of a true first-rate player. At least North Carolina has Mark Grace and Buck Leonard. South Carolina has **Dan Driessen** and **Willie Aikens**.

Driessen (b. 7/29/51 Hilton Head Island) gets the nod as the team's starter almost by virtue of his playing 15 big league seasons. He reached the big leagues in 1973, playing third base part-time for the Cincinnati Reds. That year he batted .301 in 386 at-bats with an impressive (for a rookie) on-base percentage of .347. Driessen was the Reds' starting third baseman in '74, batting .281 with little power (seven homers, 23 doubles), but lost any claim he had on third base in 1975 when Pete Rose was shifted there from left field. Driessen was consequently shifted to first base, but, unfortunately for his playing time prospects, Tony Perez was already a fixture there.

The first base job was Driessen's, though, in 1977 when Perez left for Montreal. As the Reds' everyday first baseman for the next seven years, Driessen hit as high as .300, but managed highs of only 18 home runs and .468 slugging, not exactly hallowed ground for a first baseman. Of note, he did lead all National League first basemen in fielding percentage three times, and he even paced the circuit in walks once, with 93 free passes in 1980.

The Cincinnati Reds of the 1970s were pretty good, as you may know, resulting in Driessen participating in four postseasons. He batted an inconspicuous .167 versus the Mets in the '73 NLCS, didn't play in the '75 NLCS and batted .000 in that year's World Series. His fortunes changed in 1976. After a hitless NLCS, Driessen hit .357 with a home run in the World Series, while being used primarily as a designated hitter. In the '79 NLCS he was again a non-factor, batting .083 with one walk.

Willie Mays Aikens (b. 10/14/54 Seneca) is best known as the Kansas City Royals' regular first baseman in the early 1980s, a period in which the team made two postseason appearances (1980 and '81). But Aikens may be most notorious for his public battle with drugs and his violation of baseball's substance abuse policy. In November 1983 Aikens and two Kansas City teammates—Willie Wilson and Jerry Martin—were sentenced to one year in prison for attempting to purchase cocaine. Thus Aikens became the first major leaguer to do jail time for drug charges.

Despite his personal troubles, Aikens was a player capable of hitting .302 and swatting 23 home runs ('83) or driving in 98 runs ('80). He finished his career with a modest .358 on-base percentage.

Aikens' most enduring moment may have been his performance in the 1980 World Series. In game one of the Series, Aikens blasted two two-run home runs to guide the Royals to a 7–6 victory. Three games later he again exploded for a pair of home runs in a game Kansas City won 5–3. All told, Aikens hit .400 and drove in eight runs in the six-game losing effort to the Phillies.

Second Base

The good fortune of having middle infielders who can hit a little manifests itself in South Carolina's pair of star second basemen.

Willie Randolph (b. 7/6/54 Holly Hill) played the bulk of his career (13 seasons) in the Bronx where he acted as the Yankees' sparkplug. His best season with the club came in 1980 when he led the American League in walks, 119, while batting .294 and stealing 30 bases. That year he also posted a career-high .429 on-base percentage. His 1987 season wasn't bad, either. That year he posted his highest slugging and RBI marks, .414 and 67, and batted a stellar .305.

After his inaugural season with Pittsburgh and his tenure with the Yankees, Randolph moved on to the Dodgers, A's, Brewers (where he hit a career-high .327 in 431 at-bats) and played out the string with the Mets. To Randolph's credit, he maintained his excellent strikeout-to-walk ratios through his waning years. In his last four seasons, 1989–1992 (ages 35–38), he walked 231 times and struck out only 157 times. For his career he had 1,243 walks and 675 strikeouts. That's a rate of 1.84 walks for every strikeout. Randolph also had a knack for stealing bases: He swiped 271 bases for his career.

A five-time all-star, Randolph played on seven teams destined for the playoffs, though he did not participate in the 1978 postseason due to injury. He helped propel the Yankees to five AL East titles (with two world titles) in six years, from 1976 to 1981. During that run, Randolph didn't fare well in postseason play, as he batted just .212 with no power (.328 slugging percentage).

Though perhaps not as well known as Randolph, **Del Pratt** (b. 1/10/1888 Walhalla) made a name for himself as a singles-hitting second baseman with considerable defensive skills (he led AL second basemen in putouts five times).

In 1916 Pratt's 103 runs batted in with the Browns led the AL, his first of two 100-RBI seasons. His second, in 1921 (now with the Red Sox), came on the heels of a 97-RBI campaign with the Yankees in 1920.

Despite being teammates with Babe Ruth for that 1920 season, Pratt never played for a pennant winner. It wasn't until 1921 that the Yankees went on their run of dominance. By that time, Pratt was in Boston.

Pratt finished his career with a .292 batting average and 247 stolen bases. He was a prototypical dead-ball player. He hit just 43 career homers, but his 392 doubles (with a high of 44) and 968 RBI are impressive, indeed, for a middle infielder. Pratt played 13 seasons.

Third Base

Al Rosen (b. 2/29/24 Spartanburg), the 1953 American League MVP, is one of the more unheralded all-star third basemen of all time. In his ten big-league seasons, all spent with Cleveland, Rosen led the league in home runs and runs batted in two times each. His 115 runs scored in 1953 were also tops in the AL.

Only recently has Rosen seen a couple of his unique home run records fall. In 1987 Rosen's AL rookie record for home runs was eclipsed by Mark McGwire, whose 49 were 12 more than Rosen had hit in 1950. And in 2000 Troy Glaus bettered Rosen's 47-year-old AL record for home runs by a third baseman (43) when he hit 47.

Ken Keltner, and not Rosen, was the third baseman for the 1948 Indians team that won the franchise's second and final World Series of the 20th century. Rosen was unable to supplant Keltner until 1950, by which time Rosen was 26 years old. From that time until his finger was broken in 1954 he was consistently one of the league's top players. His two post-1954 seasons, however, paled in comparison to his established level of achievement.

Rosen nearly won the triple crown in his MVP campaign. His 43 homers and 145 RBI were tops in the league, but his .336 batting average left him a mere point behind Mickey Vernon's lead. Too, Rosen paced the Junior Circuit with a .613 slugging percentage.

Though certainly not as feared a slugger as Rosen, **Red Smith** (b. 4/6/1890 Greenville) did hit a league-leading 40 doubles and 10 triples in 1913, during a period of low offensive output. His career .278 batting and .353 on-base percentages reflect well on a career spent entirely before 1920 and the advent of the livelier ball. Smith's chief ability was reaching base, as he drew 420 walks against 415 strikeouts for his career. He also stole a modest 117 bases.

In a career spent entirely in the National League with the Brooklyn Dodgers and Boston Braves, Smith did not once participate in postseason play.

This Red Smith should not be confused with his namesake Red Smith, who some rank as the preeminent baseball writer of the 20th century.

Shortstop

Marty Marion (b. 12/1/17 Richburg) is recognized as an outstanding defensive shortstop who, in his prime, could handle the bat reasonably well. Whatever your feelings on the statistic, *Total Baseball* credits Marion with 92 fielding runs, which is good but does not place him among the game's elite. (Bill Dahlen is credited with 302 fielding runs, tops among shortstops.)

On the topic of Marion's defense, Bill James had this to say in his

Historical Baseball Abstract: "One of the few players to win an MVP award almost entirely with his glove, Marion belongs somewhere in the [Dave] Bancroft–[Dick] Bartell–[Travis] Jackson–[Pee Wee] Reese–[Phil] Rizzuto line..." The MVP award to which James alluded was won by Marion in 1944 when his Cardinals beat the cross-town Browns in the World Series. It was also a season in the middle of U.S. involvement in World War II, of course, a time when many of the National League's stars were enlisted in the armed forces.

Nevertheless, Marion made one of his five appearances in the All-Star game that year, as he led all NL shortstops in fielding percentage while hitting .267 with 26 doubles. Two years earlier he had rapped a league-leading 38 doubles.

Marion drummed up strong Hall of Fame support after his career ended, as evidenced by his appearance on 14 different Hall ballots. He never won enshrinement, though, coming closest in his final appearance on the ballot, in 1973, when he received 127 votes.

Don Buddin's (b. 5/5/34 Turbeville) career lasted just six years, but in his stint as a big leaguer he mastered the art of getting on base by any means but a base hit.

A career .241 hitter, Buddin somehow managed a solid .360 on-base percentage. Coupled with his defensive abilities as a shortstop (.954 career fielding mark), Buddin's penchant for reaching base made him a valuable player in the mid–1950s and early '60s. Buddin compiled 410 bases on balls compared with 404 strikeouts for his career, and even managed to hit 41 home runs (again, in just six seasons).

Outfield

Jim Rice (b. 3/8/53 Anderson), like Ted Williams and Carl Yas-trzemski before him, patrolled Fenway Park's left field and powered the Red Sox to the World Series during his tenure. (Williams' Sox advanced to the Series in 1946, where they lost to the Cardinals; Yastrzemski's Sox lost to the Cardinals in '67 and to the Reds in '75; and Rice's Sox fell to the Mets in '86; he was injured for the '75 Series.)

While it isn't fair to compare any player to Williams or Yastrzemski, it's worth noting that Rice finished with higher career batting (.298) and slugging (.502) marks than Yastrzemski.

A seven-time All-Star, Rice three times led the American League in home runs, and two times each in RBI and slugging percentage. In his 1978 MVP campaign, Rice led all AL batters, with 46 home runs, 139 RBI, 213 hits, 15 triples and a .600 slugging percentage. He was widely considered the best player in the AL at this time, if not all of baseball. Admirable for a slugger, Rice batted over .300 six times in his career.

Rice's skills dropped off considerably after the 1986 season, at which point he was 33. Knee surgery in the 1987 off-season contributed to his decline. He batted just .263 over his last three seasons, while averaging 10 home runs and 54 runs batted in, virtually squelching any chance he had of reaching the Hall of Fame on the writers' ballot.

Joe Jackson (b. 7/16/1889 Pickens County), probably the most famous member of Team South Carolina, had the misfortune of playing in the shadow of Ty Cobb. In fact, were it not for Cobb, Shoeless Joe would probably be regarded as the best hitter of the dead ball era.

That Jackson's .356 career batting average is third best of all time, behind only Cobb (.366) and Rogers Hornsby (.358), belies the fact that Jackson did not once win a batting title, despite hitting .408 as a rookie (1911) and .395 the following year. Both times he was bested by Cobb, who hit an astonishing .420 and .410 in consecutive seasons. It is the Georgia Peach, too, who holds the batting average standards for his era and for outfielders all time. Jackson is second in both categories.

It was Jackson's distinctive left-handed swing, though, and not Cobb's, that Babe Ruth studied and patterned his own swing after.

Jackson received his first chance as a regular with Cleveland in 1911. Six years later he was on the World Series winning White Sox. He gained notoriety, though, for his role in the Black Sox scandal of 1919, in which Jackson and seven teammates threw the World Series versus the Cincinnati Reds for a reported $20,000. His role in the conspiracy earned him a lifetime ban from baseball.

Three times Jackson led the American League in triples (with a high of 26), once he led in doubles and twice he led in hits. Though he hit only 54 home runs for his career, Jackson compiled 307 doubles and 168 triples, giving him an excellent .517 slugging mark. He also stole 202 bases.

South Carolina's sole Hall of Famer, **Larry Doby** (b. 12/13/23 Camden), rounds out the stellar starting outfield corps. More than the player who integrated the American League with Cleveland in 1947, Doby was an All-Star for seven consecutive seasons on his way to 253 career home runs. He became the first black player to lead either league in home runs in 1952 with 32. With another league-leading 32 homers in 1954, Doby helped guide the Indians to the pennant and a then league-record 111 wins. He also chipped in a tops-in-circuit 126 runs batted in.

Converted to a center fielder after arriving on the big league scene as a second baseman, Doby possessed a well-rounded skill set. In addition to the home runs, Doby drew 90-plus walks six times—enabling him to finish with a .387 career on-base percentage—while batting .283 for his career.

Unlike teammate Al Rosen, Doby was established as a starter for the World Series–winning 1948 Cleveland Indians. That year, his rookie season, he batted .301 with 14 homers, 66 RBI and 23 doubles for the Tribe.

Reggie Sanders' (b. 12/1/67 Florence) name doesn't often come up when discussing the best outfielders of the 1990s, but his accomplishments merit consideration as at least one of the most well rounded.

With the ability to play any of the three outfield spots and hit for average and power, Sanders has proven his value in the middle of the lineup for the Reds, Padres, Braves and Diamondbacks with his career .350 on-base percentage and .484 slugging marks. Though the knock against Sander remains his inability to stay healthy for a full season (his career high is 138 games played), he has managed to put up some solid numbers. Through the 2001 season, his eleventh in the big leagues, he has hit 195 home runs and stolen 229 bases.

Sanders' two best seasons are fairly close statistically. In 1995 he hit .306 with 28 homers, 99 RBI, 36 doubles, 36 stolen bases, 91 runs, a .401 on-base percentage and a .579 slugging percentage for the Reds. Six years later, in Arizona, Sanders hit .263 with 33 home runs, 90 RBI, 21 doubles, 14 steals, 84 runs, a .337 on-base percentage and a .549 slugging mark.

From 1977 to 1981, **Gene Richards** (b. 9/29/53 Monticello) was a top-of-the-order force for the San Diego Padres, once stealing 61 bases in a season.

In Richards' rookie season of 1977 he got things started with a .290 average, 11 triples, 56 steals and a fine .365 on-base percentage. His best effort, though, came in 1980 when he batted .301, with 61 steals, a career-high 26 doubles and a .363 on-base percentage. Richards' 1981 season featured a league-leading 12 triples by the fleet outfielder.

Pitchers

One won't find any baseball immortals while perusing South Carolina's pitching roster. What you will find, though, is the author of a no-hitter (almost), a Cy Young award winner and eight other pitchers obscured by time and neglected by the record books.

Van Mungo (b. 6/8/11 Pageland), the Brooklyn Dodgers' ace through their lean years in the 1930s (the club was 644–729, or .469, from 1931 to 1939), is more than qualified to act as Team South Carolina's ace. He compiled a 3.47 career ERA with 115 victories.

Mungo gave the Dodgers at least 28 starts every season from 1932 through 1936, during which time he went 81–71 for a sub-.500 club. In '36 he paced the National League with 238 strikeouts. He never again would top 200 strikeouts in a season, but he had recorded 184 two years previous. Tempering the strikeout totals were plenty of walks: Mungo led the league in bases on balls issued on three occasions, issuing as many as 118 in a season. For his career, though, he was 374 to the good, with 1,242 strikeouts to 868 walks.

On two occasions Mungo pitched more than 300 innings in a season, leading the league in '34 with 315⅓. Additionally, the lanky right-hander allowed the lowest opponents' batting average in consecutive seasons, 1936–37, with marks of .234 and .229. More impressively, Mungo permitted only a .321 on-base percentage to opposing batters over the course of his career.

Bobo Newsom (b. 8/11/07 Hartsville) pitched 20 seasons for nine different teams, with the Senators acquiring him five different times and the Browns three.

Good things came in twenties for the affable Newsom. Three times in his career Newsom won 20 games. Of course, he lost 20 games three times as well. His three 20-win seasons came consecutively, from 1938 to 1940. During this time he was dealt from the Browns to the Tigers.

It was in Detroit, during the 1940 season, that Newsom was at his finest. That year his Tigers advanced to the seventh game of the World Series on the strength of his effort versus the Cincinnati Reds. Having won Games One and Five already—while giving up but two runs—Newsom pitched magnificently in a losing Game Seven effort. He had shut out the Reds through six innings when, in the seventh, Cincinnati wrestled two runs from Newsom and the Series from the Tigers. His final postseason line: two wins, one loss, a 1.38 ERA, three complete games and 17 strikeouts in 26 innings.

Also in that 1940 season, Newsom was named to his third straight All-Star team, as he was 21–5 with a 2.83 ERA during the season.

Newsom had the rare misfortune of pitching a nine-inning no-hitter only to lose the game in the extra innings. In his first full season in the major leagues, 1934, the Browns' right-hander took his hitless performance into the tenth inning before the Red Sox got to him for their first hit—and their first run. It would prove to be all they needed.

At various points in his career, Newsom led his league in complete games (twice), innings pitched and strikeouts. He was recognized as an All-Star four times.

LaMarr Hoyt (b. 1/1/55 Columbia) first experienced success as the White Sox' number one pitcher in 1982 at the age 27. By the time he was 33, Hoyt was serving a jail sentence for a series of arrests for drug possession and parole violation.

Perhaps Jack Morris and Dan Quisenberry received more recognition, but Hoyt may have been the best pitcher in the American League for the 1982 and '83 seasons. Hoyt won the Cy Young award, of course, in 1983 on the strength his 24–10 effort to help push the White Sox to the playoffs for the first time in 24 years. Detractors pointed to Hoyt's ERA of 3.66 not being among the top 15 finishers in the AL that year, but despite his merely average showing in that category, he exhibited impeccable control figures, walking just 31 batters in 260⅔ innings. He also recorded 148 strikeouts that season.

Hoyt's 1982 season featured a league-high 19 wins, a 3.53 ERA and 48 walks in 239 2/3 innings of work. After a subpar 1984 campaign, Hoyt latched on with the Padres and had mild success, going 16–8 with a 3.47 ERA. The writing was on the wall, though: Hoyt struck out just 83 batters in 210 1/3 innings. This reduced strikeout rate proved to be a predicator of his demise as a big league pitcher. He just wasn't fooling batters like he once had, and his lifestyle probably contributed to his decline. Although external circumstances had intervened, Hoyt was out of the game for good following the 1986 season.

With each successive name more memorable than the last, **Doc McJames** (b. 8/27/1873 Williamsburg) assumes his spot in the South Carolina's melodiously-monikered rotation. Though his success was fleeting, McJames was a very good pitcher for three years in his prime.

As a 22-year-old, McJames pitched 17 innings in two starts for the National League Washington Senators and surrendered only three earned runs. His 1896 season wasn't quite as productive, however, as he posted a 4.27 ERA in 33 starts and walked 32 more batters than he struck out. McJames enjoyed his finest season the following year when he led the league in strikeouts, 156, and shutouts, 3.

With a different team in 1898, the National League's Baltimore Orioles, McJames produced more of the same results. With career highs in starts and innings pitched, 42 and 374, the right-hander notched a career-best 178 strikeouts to go with his 2.36 ERA, also a high water mark. He completed all but two of his starts and won 27 games.

McJames joined the Brooklyn Superbas in 1899 and continued to pitch well. During that season he contracted malaria, however, and it forced him to cut his season a month short. At the time he was one of the top pitchers in the league with 19 wins and a 3.50 ERA. McJames missed all of the 1900 season due to the illness but eventually seemed to recover. He returned in 1901 to pitch in 13 games for the Superbas, but a relapse of the malaria forced him to leave the team and return home to South Carolina. He died on September 23 of that year, less than a month after his 28th birthday. His promising career cut tragically short, McJames had compiled 80 big-league wins in parts of six seasons, with a career 3.43 ERA.

Bobby Bolin (b. 1/29/39 Hickory Grove) boasted a ratio of nearly twice as many strikeouts (1,175) to walks (597). Though Bolin spent most of his career coming out of the bullpen, his impeccable control makes him a prime candidate for starting duty on this team. (Remember, there are no pitchers of Gaylord Perry's caliber here, though Perry and Bolin were teammates for eight seasons in San Francisco from 1962 to 1969.)

Bolin didn't start more games than he relieved until 1964, his fourth year with the Giants. At that point he had a string of three successful seasons in a row, posting ERA marks of 3.25, 2.76 and 2.89. During this stretch he also accumulated his three highest strikeout totals of 146, 135 and 143.

The South Carolina bullpen is more even in quality than is the starting rotation, but the end result is mediocrity.

Ernie White (b. 9/5/16 Pacolet Mills) pitched in just 108 big league games, amassing 30 wins in 57 career starts to go with his 2.78 ERA.

White's first four seasons, 1940–43, were spent in St. Louis at a time when the Cardinals were dominating the National League. In 1942 and '43 St. Louis squared off with the Yankees, winning the first and losing the sequel. In his first Series start (1942 Game Three), White tossed a six-hit shutout versus the Bronx Bombers, giving him an undefeated all-time Series won-lost record, 1–0, and a zero ERA. Those marks would stand through the rigors of the '43 Series as well, because White would not pitch in the five-game set. His sole appearance was as a pinch runner.

Following that 1943 season White would aid the World War II effort for the next two seasons. Upon his return in 1946 he was not the same pitcher. White made just 28 appearances in his final three seasons with the Boston Braves, just two of them starts. The left-hander was 32 years old and pitched 50⅔ innings when he played his final season in 1948. His best season was 1941 when he went 17–7 in 32 games (25 starts) and compiled a 2.40 ERA. The league batted a mere .217 against him.

Billy O'Dell (b. 2/10/32 Whitmire) won 105 games in his career, despite spending the bulk of his 13-year tenure pitching out of the bullpen (where he saved 48 games). Like Bolin, O'Dell was teammate to Gaylord Perry with the Giants in the early 1960s.

He came up with the Orioles, though, and it was there that he was twice named an All-Star, in 1958 and '59. Those years the left-hander posted sparkling 2.97 and 2.93 ERA marks in consecutive seasons.

One of O'Dell's finest seasons coincided with one of the San Francisco Giants' finest. The 1962 Giants won the National League pennant, while O'Dell won a career high 19 games in a career-high 39 starts with a career-high 195 strikeouts.

With the Milwaukee Braves three years after that, O'Dell posted a 2.18 ERA, a mark he would not better in his career. O'Dell's starting days were over, however, and he saw action in 111⅓ innings.

It was his versatility and his ability to compile innings (whether starting or relieving), though, that ultimately made O'Dell a valuable pitcher. The fact that he could keep his pitches in the strike zone didn't hurt, either. He tossed 1,817 innings for his career, striking out 1,133 and walking 556. More numbers: O'Dell started 199 games in his career and relieved 280 others.

The Seattle Pilots lasted for exactly one season, 1969. **Dooley Womack** (b. 8/25/39 Columbia) got in on the action in the Emerald City, albeit for just nine games.

Womack was an effective reliever for five years, sure, but more than that, his name was immortalized by its appearance in Jim Bouton's landmark book, *Ball Four*. From World Series hero with the Yankees to Seattle Pilot, Bouton had converted to a knuckleball pitcher after his career had reached a standstill. An arm injury had cost him his fastball and his form. In a turbulent '69 season that saw him farmed out to Vancouver at one point, Bouton was mercifully traded from the Pilots to the Houston Astros in August.

Upon learning of the trade, Bouton wonders whom he has been swapped for. The answer, of course, is Womack. It isn't flattering, but this is how I'll always remember Dooley Womack. From *Ball Four*: "I hope there was a lot of undisclosed cash involved [in the trade].... Maybe it's me for a hundred thousand and Dooley Womack is just a throw-in. I'd hate to think that at this stage of my career I was being traded even-up for Dooley Womack." Contrary to Bouton's bluster, at that point in their careers Womack *was* a superior pitcher. Womack had compiled a 3.51 ERA with the Astros in 30 games prior to the trade. (Bouton was at 3.91 prior to the trade.) For good measure, Womack went 2–1 with a 2.51 ERA for the Pilots after the trade.

Womack started one game as a major leaguer. His other 192 appearances were in relief, where he finished with a 2.95 ERA and 177 strikeouts in 302 1/3 innings of work. Inconspicuous but effective, Womack pitched for the Yankees and A's, in addition to the aforementioned Astros and Pilots.

Bill Landrum (b. 8/17/57 Columbia) was at his best as a right-handed setup man for the National League East–winning Pittsburgh Pirates of 1990 and '91.

Though not a strikeout pitcher, Landrum found other ways to get batters out. In 1990, his finest season, he posted a 2.13 ERA coming out of the Pirates' 'pen, though he struck out just 39 in 71⅔ innings and allowed a .262 opponents' batting average. The '91 season was similar in that his ERA was again superb (3.18), while his peripheral statistics were on par: 45 strikeouts in 76⅓ innings with a .252 opponents' average. As productive as those years were, Landrum's best may have actually been 1989, when he posted a 1.67 ERA in 56 appearances.

Landrum started two major league games over the course of his eight-year career spent with the Cubs, Pirates, Expos and Reds. He finished with a 3.39 ERA.

Toiling with mediocre clubs for the length of his career, **Art Fowler** (b. 7/3/22 Converse) never saw action in the postseason.

A spot starter for his first three seasons with the Reds, Fowler fared well in this capacity, but not so much as to keep him from full relief duty in the future. As a 31-year-old rookie in 1954 he won 12 games for the fifth-place Reds. His ERA was 3.83, but that would rise the next two seasons as his win totals dropped and held at 11 both years.

Though he would never again start more than seven games in a season for the balance of his nine-year career, Fowler was durable. In those non-starting years he would appear in 33, 36, 53, 48, 57 and, finally, four games. During that period he twice sported an ERA under three. For the Dodgers, in 1962, Fowler finished at 2.81 with four relief wins and an opponents' batting average of .234.

His next season in Dodger blue was even better than his first. In '63 Fowler won five games to go with a career-best 2.42 ERA and a career-most 89⅓ relief innings.

Alas, Fowler pitched in just seven games the following year for Los Angeles (to the tune of a 10.29 ERA) and unceremoniously exited the baseball stage.

Determining roster constitution consistent with today's accepted practices and roles made choosing the All-North and All–South Carolina Teams fun and at least a little relevant to fans. But it offers another, more subtle benefit. The passage of time has eradicated all memory of Cliff

Melton and Don Buddin to all but the biggest baseball history buffs or the most fanatical team followers. With the completion of both North and South Carolina teams, these players, along with other members of baseball's forgotten fraternity, whether they be Bill Landrum or Pep Young, have garnered recognition for their accomplishments on the baseball field.

Pitching Staff

Starters	Won-Lost	Pct.	ERA	Seasons	Years Active
Van Mungo, rhp	120–115	.511	3.47	14	1931–45
Bobo Newsom, rhp	211–222	.487	3.98	20	1929–53
LaMarr Hoyt, rhp	98–68	.590	3.99	8	1979–86
Doc McJames, rhp	79–80	.497	3.43	6	1895–1901
Bobby Bolin, rhp	88–75	.540	3.40	13	1961–73

Relievers	Won-Lost	Saves	ERA	Seasons	Years Active
Ernie White, lhp	30–21	6	2.78	7	1940–48
Billy O'Dell, lhp	105–100	48	3.29	13	1954–67
Bill Landrum, rhp	18–15	58	3.39	8	1986–93
Dooley Womack, rhp	19–18	24	2.95	5	1966–70
Art Fowler, rhp	54–51	32	4.03	9	1954–64

Position Players

Lineup	Bats	Avg.	OBP	SLG	HR	Seasons	Years Active
Willie Randolph, 2b	R	.276	.375	.351	54	18	1975–92
Joe Jackson, rf	L	.356	.423	.517	54	13	1908–20
Larry Doby, cf	L	.283	.387	.490	253	13	1947–59
Jim Rice, lf	R	.298	.356	.502	382	16	1974–89
Al Rosen, 3b	R	.285	.386	.495	192	10	1947–56
Dan Driessen, 1b	L	.267	.359	.411	153	15	1973–87
Aaron Robinson, c	L	.260	.375	.412	61	8	1943–51
Marty Marion, ss	R	.263	.323	.345	36	13	1940–53

Bench	Bats	Avg.	OBP	SLG	HR	Seasons	Years Active
Mickey Livingston, c	R	.238	.310	.326	19	10	1938–51
Willie Aikens, 1b	L	.271	.358	.455	110	8	1977–85
Del Pratt, 2b	R	.292	.345	.403	43	13	1912–24
Red Smith, 3b	R	.278	.353	.377	27	9	1911–19
Don Buddin, ss	R	.241	.360	.359	41	6	1956–62
Reggie Sanders, of	R	.268	.350	.484	195	11	1991–present
Gene Richards, of	L	.290	.358	.383	26	8	1977–84

Baseball: The Heart and Mind of America

by David Beal

I was born in December of 1941 and grew up in a time when information and news about life's happenings were gained by searching for them. Radio and newspapers provided most of what I knew about the world in my early years, and only in the 1950s did the miracle of television arrive, with its instant picture and sound of the world around us. The search for what was going on in the world was serious, and sometimes no matter how hard you tried, instant information remained beyond your grasp.

Enter baseball. Young and old alike could tell you instantly what team they pulled for in the major and minor leagues. Most everyone had a favorite player, or hero, that they followed. Although World War II had interrupted the whole world, people in the late '40s and early '50s were anxious to put that horror behind them and think pleasant thoughts. Having baseball to follow occupied the minds of people everywhere, especially mine.

I was lucky. My uncle, Bobby Beal, was a professional baseball player

David Beal, a former SBI Agent and retired Clerk of Superior Court, has served as volunteer Special Assistant to the General Manager of the Winston-Salem Warthogs for the past 12 years.

Rube Walker's 1958 baseball card.
(Courtesy of Chris Holaday.)

who spent most of his career in the minor leagues of the South. Cities like Charlotte, Memphis, Augusta and Chattanooga opened up to me each summer as we went to see him play. Also, my hometown of Lenoir, like many smaller towns of that era, had its own team. Ours was a Class D farm club of the Boston Red Sox. The sandwich board sign would appear in the middle of the traffic circle during the summer announcing "BASEBALL TONITE" and we would all come alive.

On game nights when I was the batboy for my uncle's teams, the Lincolnton Cardinals or Marion Marauders, the sights and sounds of baseball were everywhere. Instructions from the manager consisted of "Don't let the bats get crossed, it's bad luck," or "Don't ever say that a pitcher has a no-hitter going." On a bus trip between towns in the Western Carolina League my uncle sat me in the door well of the bus and told me to count the white horses in the fields as we passed. "Every white horse is a base hit," he said, so I counted intently and reported my total.

Pay for the batboy was usually an old ball or a broken bat. One night, after an especially thrilling comeback win, the players on the team took up a collection and paid me $5.00. I thought I was rich and the next day went to the hardware store, bought a new glove, and even had some money left over.

But then there was the jewel in the crown: a real-life major league baseball player, born, raised and living in Lenoir during the off-season. Albert Bluford "Rube" Walker, a catcher for the Chicago Cubs (1948–1951) and the Brooklyn Dodgers (1951–1958), was our hero in Caldwell and surrounding counties. In the midst of post-war America, Korean conflicts and a catastrophic polio epidemic, we had Rube. Nothing in the world could equal the feeling of pride we had in following Rube's statistics in the paper, owning his Topps baseball card, or actually talking to him in person in the off-season. Who could resist the stories he told about playing in the major leagues, or being on the cover of the September 4, 1949, edition of the *Saturday Evening Post* in Norman Rockwell's now famous "The Dugout." Rube had been "beaned" that afternoon by a pitch, causing Rockwell to give him the original cardboard sketch of the drawing that would appear on the cover.

Although he didn't talk about it much, there was also October 3, 1951, now famous in baseball history for the "Shot Heard 'Round the World." The Dodgers and Giants were in a playoff for the National League pennant. The Dodgers were ahead in the bottom of the ninth, with Bobby Thomson at bat for the Giants and Ralph Branca on the mound for the "bums." But do you know who was catching for the Dodgers? Roy Campanella, of course. Not so—it was Rube Walker. Campanella was hurt and Rube had been called on in his backup role to catch. The rest is history, and as Rube would later say: "Me and Branca, we were like a couple of lepers. I called it, he threw it. Nobody wanted to come near us." And to think I heard it firsthand from the man who was there.

Historian Jacques Barzun said in 1954, "Whoever wants to know the heart and mind of America had better learn baseball." Baseball is full of great moments, moods, frustrations and memories. Americans have been accused of forgetting how to have fun and make memories, but if that is true, we are doomed. I believe that baseball truly is the heart and mind of America, particularly here in the Carolinas. Because of it I will continue to have fun and make memories. I hope that you will too.

South Carolina
and the AAGPBL

---

by Robert H. Gaunt

The role of baseball around South Carolina's mill towns, and tales of the hotly contested games that were part of every summer's way of life over a half century ago, are fairly well known. Less attention has been paid to the women's softball leagues that shared the summer spotlight during the mid–twentieth century, and in particular to some of the talented players who were a part of those operations. Elizabeth "Lib" Mahon, who grew up in a mill village located directly across the street from the Brandon Mill, was among the most talented of those who ever played on the diamonds that were usually the property of one of the area's many textile mills.

It wasn't easy for a female ball player to hone her diamond skills in the thirties. The high schools did not offer athletic programs for female students, but Lib liked playing ball and could often be seen "out there with the boys" during a great many hot Upstate summer afternoons. "My mother used to worry about me," Lib declares. "She used to say, 'Elizabeth, what are folks going to think about your hanging around with boys

---

A retired college professor and Coast Guard officer, Robert Gaunt is the author of We Would Have Played Forever: The Story of the Coastal Plain Baseball League. *He can usually be found residing in either Maggie Valley, NC, or Hilton Head, SC.*

all the time.'" But she assures that things were always on the up and up. "If any of them tried to use bad language, or began sounding improper in any way, I'd take my equipment and go home. That would usually break up the game, because I usually owned the ball."

Brandon Mill didn't have a girls' team, but Lib's reputation as a talented player spread, and when she was twelve she was recruited to play on a softball team consisting mostly of adults who were employed at a mill which was located "across town." A team representative would drive to Lib's Brandon home, pick her up, transport her to the

Lib Mahon. (Photograph courtesy of Jim Sargent.)

game, and then return her home afterwards. "It was a new car," she reported, "and there weren't many new cars around in those Depression days." During the winter months she played on the basketball teams that were also part of the textile mill recreation network. Basketball for girls, back in the early days, was a game played by six player–teams, each team having three defenders and three offensive players who were confined to opposite ends of the court. Needless to say, contests had only a scant resemblance to the game that is currently played by female teams all over the country.

Mahon was a good student during her high school days, but life wasn't particularly carefree for youngsters living in mill towns during the latter stages of the Great Depression. "We were poor folks. Poor but proud, as my mother used to say," Mahon says. Part of a big family, Lib decided to take a job in the Brandon Mill while completing her senior year in high school. "I would go to school until three, and then I would report to the mill for my work, and that lasted until midnight. The next day I would be up, and it was time to head back to classes." It was a tough life, but the $8–10 per week that came in the pay envelope was very helpful in a household where everyone worked hard to do their parts in helping to keep the Mahon family afloat.

Even though life at the mill meant 55-hour weeks for those who were considered full-time employees, girls' athletic teams usually were made up of employees who held jobs at their respective plants. Games were normally played on weekends, though an occasional weekday game came into the picture from time to time. "We were a bit limited in terms of how many games we could play because we would simply get too tired to carry on all the rest of our responsibilities," reports Mahon. While it was common practice for men's mill teams to put talented ball players on the local payroll to shore up the strength of their lineup, Mahon was not aware of any similar practices being used by any of the female teams in her area. "We just played for fun," she says, "and we drew pretty good crowds. Sometimes we'd have a thousand or even two thousand people out there for one of our games." Despite being one of the better players around the entire Greenville area, which had "10 to 12" mill teams, Lib never received payment for playing on any of those teams.

The team's ball schedules had to be completed on weekdays and on Saturdays. "Sunday was the Sabbath, and it was considered a sin to play on Sundays," Mahon reports. "That was how the Southern Baptists saw things in those days, and I guess that they still think along those same lines down in those parts." The Sunday ball-playing issue was one that was a very controversial subject and hotly debated in many Southern towns, especially when significant numbers of minor league teams were being established following the War Years; and it appears that sentiments in South Carolina's Upstate were not immune from those battles.

Mahon continued to work at her "boring, boring" mill job following her graduation and had figured that she'd spend her working years in that environment, but an aunt offered to pay the costs if she'd agree to enroll at Winthrop College. Thrilled to have an opportunity to secure a college education, Lib quickly accepted the generous proposition. Winthrop, located in Rock Hill, SC, was then an all-girls college, and Lib began her freshman year on the campus in the fall of 1938.

There were no intercollegiate teams at Winthrop at the time, but there was always a spirited competition between the various classes for superiority in field hockey, basketball, and softball. Lib quickly found prominent roles in those activities, and she proudly remembers days when her class teams "beat the seniors"—a feat which was considered very significant for an underclass team back in that era.

Lib's studies led her to become an educator, and when she graduated from Winthrop she returned to the Greenville area and began an assignment as a high school teacher. Though it was a step up from life in the mill, her $90 monthly paycheck wasn't really allowing her to make ends meet. After one year, and somewhat sadly, she resigned her teaching position to take a job with the Post Office. It wasn't what she'd had in mind while studying during her college years, but the pay was a bit better and a job with the Post Office was then considered a steady and dependable assignment. She had also resumed her summer ball playing. A good hitter and a versatile talent who was able to handle several positions, Mahon was considered one of the area's premier players.

During the War Years the women's leagues drew even more attention than usual. That was due to the shortage of talented male ball players (owing to the fact that most of the country's young men were wearing some sort of military uniform). Top-flight women's leagues were still operating, while many of the men's leagues became filled with older players or else went out of business for the "duration." It was during World War II that Chicago chewing gum magnate Phillip Wrigley became sold on the idea of establishing the first women's professional league. President Franklin D. Roosevelt provided added momentum when he proclaimed that baseball was part of the American fabric, and that baseball should continue to be played as a means of maintaining civilian morale during the difficult War Years.

Thus, in 1943, the All-American Girls Baseball League was founded, beginning in four Midwestern towns. It proved to be a success, and when the 1944 season was being planned, Wrigley decided it was time to add a couple of additional teams to the league's lineup. That created a need for enough players to establish the expansion teams, bringing an opportunity for Lib Mahon.

As is so often the case in similar situations, Mahon's opportunity came when someone who had seen her play passed along a tip to a league official. In her case it was Jimmy Gaston, the president of the Greenville Spinners, a prominent local minor league baseball team. Gaston had traveled to Nashville and had met an official from the All-American League. When he was informed that the league was conducting a talent search, the

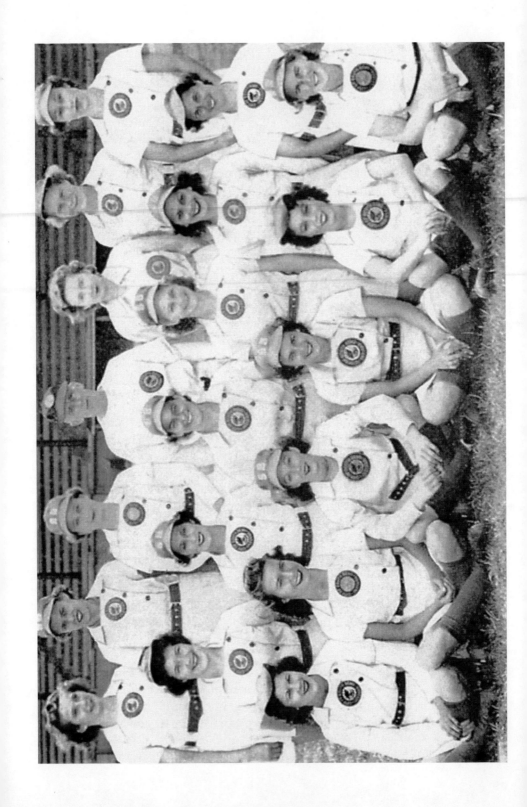

eventual result was that Mahon and one of her teammates, Viola "Tommy" Thompson, were offered the opportunity to come to the league's tryouts, which were to be held in Chicago. With the prospect of making the $60 per week that was being paid to members of the established teams, the two Greenville girls decided to try their hand in the new league.

"We were just a couple of bumpkins, and neither one of us had ever been more than 100 miles from home," recalled Mahon as she remembered their northward journey. "The train wasn't air conditioned in those days, and it was hot, so we had to ride up there with the windows down. We were dirty, tired and full of soot when we arrived in Chicago, and then we missed our connection to the area where we were supposed to go. And then it was four in the morning when we finally arrived and we had to go to tryouts at ten o'clock." Mahon remembers feeling a bit overwhelmed as she watched the competition for the forty or so jobs that were up for grabs at the camp. "I had never seen so many talented players," she declared. "I thought I wouldn't make it. I had come with the idea that I was a pretty fair ball player, but when I saw that crowd, I began to feel quite average."

But both Mahon and Thompson managed to win full-time jobs in the new league. Mahon was assigned to the Minneapolis Millerettes, a franchise that didn't last long in the All-American League, and she eventually finished her first season as a member of the Kenosha Comets. Playing in the outfield and taking an occasional turn at one of the infield spots, Mahon quickly established herself as a solid player who was assured of an opportunity to return for the 1945 season. Thompson, in the meantime, was assigned to the Milwaukee Chicks, a team that was relocated to Grand Rapids for the 1945 season. A left-handed pitcher, Thompson was relied upon heavily by the Chicks, and she posted a 15–23 mark while tossing a hefty 310 innings for her not-very-successful ball club.

There is an interesting footnote to the story of South Carolina's role in the AAGPBL. Tommy Thompson had a sister, Freda Acker, who was reportedly a fairly respectable ball player in her own right; but, perhaps more importantly, in 1947 she was the reigning Mrs. America. The mother of a two-year-old son, Acker was signed to a contract with the South Bend Blue Sox and brought to the league's Spring Training camp which was held, that year, in Havana, Cuba. Though Acker never got into an actual game with the Sox, she was utilized as an instructor in an exercise the

Opposite: The 1946 South Bend Blue Sox. Lib Mahon is on the back row, far right. Viola Thompson is on the front row, second from left. (Photograph courtesy of Jim Sargent.)

league called "charm training," and she was prominently featured in the league's Spring Training "fashion show." The only other South Carolina player associated with the league was a pitcher from Georgetown whose name was Esther Johnson. Little is known about Johnson, but her stay with the league was limited to a very short period spent with the South Bend Blue Sox.

Tommy Thompson remained in the league for a couple of additional seasons before returning to South Carolina to marry and settle in the Upstate region. Mahon, on the other hand, stayed around for a total of nine seasons in the All-American League. Along the way she was chosen to the league's All Star team on two occasions, and she became the All-American's second highest runs-batted-in leader. Her 72 runs batted in during the 1946 season, while playing for the South Bend Blue Sox, stood as the league record until it was eclipsed four years later. During that same season she was credited for stealing 114 bases out of 116 attempts. "The catchers couldn't throw," she modestly remembers. "I didn't even have to slide most of the time.

Lib Mahon quit playing during the 1952 season. The league had begun to go downhill as interest in the novelty of top-flight women's baseball was losing its luster; and baseball, in general, was beginning to fall on harder times. But it wasn't a matter of the league not doing quite as well as it had been during earlier years. Instead, it was a matter of principle that finally drove her into an early retirement. "We had a manager that we really weren't fond of," she says. "And when he fined one of our younger players $100 for something that she'd done, several of us veterans felt that he was being too harsh, so we went to see him and told him how we felt." One hundred dollars amounted to a week's pay at that time, and while no one objected to paying five dollars for missing a call or something like that, the six veteran players felt that the manager's penalty just wasn't a fair one. When he refused to budge and stubbornly stood by his decision, the team's veteran players walked out of the room, gathered their belongings, and left the team. That was the end of Lib Mahon's All-American career.

Unlike Tommy Thompson, Lib did not return to South Carolina. Instead, she accepted a teaching position in the South Bend Public School System, where she remained as a teacher and later a guidance counselor until her retirement in 1981. "They paid teachers about $2,000 more in Indiana than they did in South Carolina," she says, "and that gave me the opportunity to spend my working years doing what I had trained to do." In addition, after eight years of playing for the local South Bend Blue Sox, she had a network of friends and favorite places in the Northern Indiana city where she continues to reside. "I've had a good life," she says, "but I still think of myself as a South Carolina girl."

The AAGPBL went out of business in the mid-fifties, but there is now a permanent display at the Baseball Hall of Fame that honors those who were part of what was a remarkable operation. In 1992 Hollywood produced the movie *A League of Their Own*, which was a fictionalized account of activities in the All-American Girl's Professional Baseball League. Starring Tom Hanks and Geena Davis, the film brought a brief bit of attention to the old league, and it prompted a round of reunions and times spent remembering the days when the league flourished. The AAGPBL was actually many years ahead of its time, and there are more than a few historians who consider the league's players as pioneers in the important movement which has eventually brought women's athletics to the prominent place it occupies a half century later. South Carolinians can justly be proud that a small group of daughters of the Palmetto State played a significant role in helping to advance women's athletics during those early years.

A Death of Innocence

by Thomas K. Perry

The Anderson County League Baseball Championship series between Chiquola and Gluck cotton mills began on Saturday, September 1, 1934, with the latter team hosting the first two games in Anderson. The Chicks swept past the home nine 6–4 in the opener, and Gluck evened the series with a 10–9 win in the Wednesday, September 5 slugfest. The third contest was scheduled at Chiquola in Honea Path the following Saturday. Things didn't go as planned.

Labor strife had edged toward the boiling point for several weeks, and it finally erupted at Chiquola over issues of pay, workloads, and concerns over the treatment of the mill workers by the owners. On September 6, during the morning shift change, tempers were short and the atmosphere was ripe for a brawl. No one, though, was prepared for the magnitude of what was to come.

Labor loyalists from nearby mills (which were closed due to strikes), and "flying squadrons" (armed union supporters riding flatbed trucks

---

Tom Perry's hitting ability, from Little League through Legion, established the parameters for the Mendoza line—and he didn't even get credit for it.

Opposite: A mid–1930s Chiquola Mill team (probably 1935). Catcher Al Evans, at the far left on the front row, went on to have a long big league career. (Photograph courtesy of the late Cecil Tyson.)

Championship Game

ANDERSON COUNTY TEXTILE LEAGUE

(Three Out of Five Games.)

Saturday, September 1st, 1934

GLUCK MILL PARK

Wednesday, September 5th Game In Anderson.

Saturday, September 8th Game in Honea Path.

(Courtesy of Thomas Perry.)

from location to location) joined with local members against employees loyal to the company. There were taunts and fist-fights, and when a single shot was fired, all hell broke loose. In a three-minute barrage of bullets, it was over. Six men were dead, and twelve men and one woman were wounded on what would be forever known as Bloody Thursday. Each side accused the other of firing that first lethal shot.

Because of the bloodshed and death only two days removed, and out of respect for the families touched by this tragedy, the Chicks felt it best to forfeit the series. Records show that Gluck Mill captured the 1934 crown, but in reality it has remained the championship that was never played.

The 1947 Albemarle League Playoffs

by Parker Chesson

As it did in other parts of the country, the popularity of baseball in Northeastern North Carolina returned with a vengeance after World War II. To bring the game back to that part of the state, the semi-pro Albemarle League was hastily reorganized in the late spring of 1946. Originally founded in 1930, the Albemarle League had been forced to fold in the mid–1930s by the lingering effects of the Great Depression.

In 1946, however, the new Albemarle League was a big success in the small towns of Northeastern North Carolina. Elizabeth City, Edenton, Hertford, Camden, Windsor, and Colerain played a fifty-game schedule, with the Edenton Colonials defeating the Windsor Rebels in four straight games to win the championship playoffs.

The results of 1946 showed there was strong fan support for summer baseball, and when 1947 rolled around, the Albemarle League again had six members—Elizabeth City, Hertford, Edenton, Windsor, Colerain, and Suffolk. Camden had dropped out and was replaced by the Suffolk

---

Parker Chesson, a native of Hertford, North Carolina, grew up across the road from Jim "Catfish" Hunter. The Hunter boys, the Chesson boys, and the nearby Nixon boys played together and had their own community baseball team. Boston Red Sox right fielder Trot Nixon's father, Billy, was one of those youngsters.

Red Sox from just across the state line in Southeastern Virginia. With crowds of over 1000 common, the league proved to be even more successful.

Fans poured into the ballparks to see games, particularly those played at night since many of them were farm people who were unable to attend afternoon games. When the championship playoffs started between the Edenton Colonials and the Colerain Trappers, attendance skyrocketed. Old-timers in that part of the state still talk about that series and the hordes of spectators that descended upon Edenton and Colerain. Never was fan interest higher or the rivalry more intense.

The Edenton Colonials walked away from the other five teams during the regular season, winning 43 of a 60-game schedule. The Colerain Trappers came in second, winning 35 games. The Hertford Indians and the Suffolk Red Sox came in third and fourth, respectively. At the end of the season, the Albemarle League used the Shaughnessy playoff format, in which the top four teams in the league had playoffs to determine the champion. This kept fan interest and attendance high—and gave the teams additional revenue.

In the semifinal playoffs, pennant-winner Edenton defeated Hertford four games to one, advancing to the championship series. Colerain swept Suffolk in four straight games. The stage was set for what turned out to be a knockdown, drag-out seven-game series between the Edenton Colonials and the Colerain Trappers. These seven games are still talked about today by the players and the fans that saw them. It is not uncommon to hear an old-timer say, "Do you remember that final game between Edenton and Colerain in 1947?"

Never before or since has a series of baseball games or any other athletic event in that rural part of North Carolina caused the intense interest as did this championship series played during the first nine days of September in 1947. These two teams were natural rivals. Edenton, an historic town on the east shore of the Chowan River, dwarfed the crossroads community of Colerain that was located on the western banks of the same river. Prior to 1947, dating back to the turn of the century, Edenton had fielded very competitive baseball teams. Baseball interest continued after 1947 as well. In 1951 the town entered true professional baseball for the first time when the Edenton Colonials joined the Class D Virginia League. In 1952, after the Virginia League folded, the Edenton club switched to the Class D Coastal Plain League. Surprisingly, Edenton won the championship playoffs that year—and then that league folded.

Colerain was a very small community in 1947, with a population of around 300. For most of the first half of the twentieth century it was the

center of herring fishing in that region. Over fifty years later, its population remains about the same and the fishing industry is practically dead.
But this small community, incorporated in 1794, has always taken great
pride in its history and its place in the Albemarle region. In the years following World War II, baseball enthusiasts in Colerain were determined
to field a competitive team in the Albemarle League.

In 1947 the Albemarle League teams were allowed to hire up to five
non-resident players. Edenton, Colerain, and the other teams were well
stocked with star players from North Carolina State College, Wake Forest College, Duke University, and the University of North Carolina. The
All-Star Team selected by a vote of the fans at the end of the 1947 season
had eight of the 11 named All-Stars being from NC State, Wake Forest,
and UNC. Two of the other three All-Stars were former professional players. Bill Fowler, a native of Charlotte, NC, and a star at NC State, played
for Colerain during the summers of 1947, '48 and '49. He recalls being
paid $350 per month, plus being put up with several other players in a
beach cottage about a mile from the ballpark. They were even furnished
meals, with a maid cooking for them and cleaning the cottage. Local players were not paid, though it was not uncommon for the hat to be passed
near the end of a game. The proceeds would go to players who had starred
in that game, or fans would give them "fence money"—bills pushed
through the protective wire in front of the grandstand.

The Edenton Colonials lineup included two league All-Stars, outfielder Trot Leary and right-handed pitcher Lester Jordan. Both were
natives of Chowan County. At 31 years of age, Leary was older than most
of the other players. Though he had never played professionally, numerous fans and former Albemarle League players state that he was one of the
most talented hitters and fielders in the league. Leary died of Lou Gehrig's
disease in 1974, but baseball ability continues to run in his family: his
great-nephew, Trot Nixon, is now the right fielder for the Boston Red
Sox. Lester Jordan was also older than most of the college players since
he had played professionally for several years. He had advanced as high
as the AAA Toronto Maple Leafs of the International League, but after
getting into a salary dispute he was released and returned to his hometown to play in the Albemarle League.

The 1947 Colerain Trappers featured four members of the league's
All-Star team, three of them college players hired for the summer. Bill
Fowler, from NC State, played centerfield. A powerful clutch hitter, Fowler
would be a standout in the championship series. Russ Batchelor, from
Wake Forest, was the Trappers' catcher. Vinnie Dilorenzo, a lanky left-
hander from UNC, was the Trappers' star pitcher during the season and

the championship series. Second baseman Frank Sangalli was a former professional player.

Game one of the championship series was played under the lights on Hicks Field in Edenton on Labor Day, September 1. Hicks Field, with a seating capacity of about 1,500, was built as a WPA project in 1939. (Interestingly, Hicks Field has recently been restored and is now listed on the National Register of Historic Places.) On that hot September night in 1947, approximately 3,000 fans saw Edenton edge Colerain 2–1 in a ten-inning game. Fans were crammed into every nook and cranny of the ballpark, with standing fans lining the foul lines. Pitcher Herman Vick of the Colonials allowed only three hits and scored the winning run in the bottom of the tenth inning. Ernie Johnson, a star hurler from NC State, pitched for Colerain and surrendered only five hits.

The next night, Colerain came back to Edenton for the second game. For this contest the visitors sent ace lefthander Vinnie Dilorenzo to the mound. Thanks to a devastating curve ball, he pitched a masterful game and, in front of 2,300 fans, blanked the Colonials 2–0 on three scattered hits. In doing so, he bested Edenton's Lester Jordan, who allowed only four hits himself. Colerain's centerfielder, Bill Fowler, got two of those hits and played brilliantly in the field. Trot Leary connected for two of Edenton's three hits.

On Wednesday afternoon at 3:30 p.m. the scene switched to Colerain. Because the Trappers didn't have lights on their field, only this third game would be played in the town. The people of Colerain had probably never seen such a crowd, as it filled every available space in the ballpark, including along the foul lines and all the way to the fence. Newspaper accounts of that game state that 1,800 fans were shoehorned into the tiny ballpark—and what a game they saw. Colerain went into the top of the ninth inning leading 6–5. Trot Leary came to bat with two out and a man on first. He smashed a towering home run over the centerfield fence to give the Colonials a 7–6 lead. In the bottom of the ninth, outstanding defensive play held the lead for the visitors. Bill Fowler again led the hitting for Colerain, going four for five, but it wasn't enough and Edenton now had a two-games-to-one edge in the series.

The next night Colerain was back in Edenton, with the first game

Opposite: The 1947 Colerain Trappers. *Kneeling:* Morgan "Lefty" Magee, Lagray "Poss" Askew, Mofield Evans, Bill Fowler, Vernon "Preacher" Mustian. *Standing:* J. C. Evans, Shirley Fairless, Vinnie Dilorenzo, Fred Castelloe, Frank Sangalli, Ed Daniels, Ernie Johnson, Russ Batchelor, Rudy Castelloe. (Photograph courtesy of Bill Fowler.)

pitchers, Vick for Edenton and Johnson for Colerain, opposing each other again. This time it was not even close. The Trappers blasted the Colonials 15–1 before 3,200 fans. Ernie Johnson allowed only six hits, and Fowler had another great night, going four for six and hitting two homers. Now the series was knotted at two games apiece.

On Friday night, again in Edenton before an even larger crowd of nearly 3,500, the two teams faced off for the fifth time. They played for eleven innings, with Edenton Manager John Byrum blasting a three-run homer in the bottom of the eleventh to win the game for his Colonials, 7–4. Dilorenzo was the loser and Lester Jordan picked up the win in relief of starter J. D. Thorne. With this win, Edenton again took the lead in the series, three games to two.

At this point, the weather played to Colerain's advantage. The Saturday night game was rained out and a game was not scheduled for Sunday, giving both teams a much-needed two-day rest. At this point, five tough games had been played in five days, two of them going into extra innings. As it turned out, the two days of rest seemed to help Colerain's pitching staff.

On Monday night, September 8, Edenton and Colerain were back under the lights on Hicks Field, this time before a crowd of close to 4,000. Trappers' pitcher Ernie Johnson was in and out of trouble all night, allowing nine hits. Good defensive play and bearing down with men on base allowed Johnson to win by a score of 3–2. Each team now had three wins, and once more the series was tied.

The seventh and deciding game of the series was high drama. Edenton had its ace, right-handed Lester Jordan, rested and ready. Colerain had its ace, lefty Vinnie Dilorenzo, equally prepared. And the fans were certainly ready as they poured into Edenton from all directions. Between 4,000 and 4,500 jammed Hicks field, filling the grandstand, the bleachers, and the temporary seating that had been brought in. Fans lined the foul lines and even ringed the distant parts of the outfield. This was undoubtedly the largest crowd to ever assemble in that part of the state, certainly for an athletic event. Long time sports observers in that region say they had never seen anything like it—nor have they seen such a crowd since. Highway patrolmen were called in to direct the traffic and to untangle traffic jams on the streets close to Hicks Field.

The stage was properly set for a showdown between these two across-the-river rivals. Both Jordan and Dilorenzo pitched well, but the Colerain hurler did just a little better. While his jaw worked a huge wad of chewing gum, Dilorenzo's left arm allowed only three hits and stuck out eight to win his second game of the series. Fowler went two for four, ending the series with fifteen hits and four homers. When the last man was out, the Colerain Trappers had defeated the Edenton Colonials 3–0, winning the 1947 championship of the Albemarle League.

The 1947 seven-game championship series stands out as the high point in the history of the Albemarle League. The seven-game series had attracted about 22,000 fans. For comparison, in 1952, when the Edenton Colonials beat the Goldsboro Jets for the championship of the professional Coastal Plain League on the same Hicks Field, a crowd of only about 1,700 attended the game. The Colonials total home attendance that year was slightly over 24,000 for sixty-two games. Obviously, interest in small-town baseball was rapidly declining in Northeastern North Carolina, just as it was all across the country. A mere five years before, fans had been incredibly enthusiastic in their support of area baseball, particularly the fast and competitive brand of the game that was played in the Albemarle League.

Vinnie Dilorenzo got to the AAA level in the New York Giants organization and came close to being called up to the big leagues late in the 1951 season. A broken wrist on his throwing arm ended his career. Dilorenzo, in a recent interview, said, "The 1947 seven-game playoffs was one of the highlights of my baseball career, right up there with a couple of no-hitters I pitched. The crowd at that last game was simply amazing. Fans were everywhere and the noise they made was really something." Though he never went back to Colerain after that season, he has very fond memories of the summer of 1947.

Bill Fowler met his future wife that summer, Colerain native Hazel Sessoms. After finishing college, he played professionally for several years (including stints with Raleigh and Fayetteville in the Carolina League), but eventually settled in Colerain and retired after over thirty years in the local school system, most of those as a school principal. In a recent interview he talked at length about the 1947 playoffs. After the last game in Edenton, the Colerain players and fans went back across the Chowan River to nearby Colerain Beach, where they had a huge celebration. "We were fed all we wanted, we had fireworks, and we really had a happy time. It was one of the most memorable nights of my baseball career," said Fowler.

Colerain's ballpark has been gone for many years, being replaced by an elementary school. But the old-timers still have vivid memories of those days when baseball was the center of community life.

Judge Lew

by Hank Utley and Chris Holaday

In the summer of 1922, as Manly Llewellyn stood on the pitcher's mound at Yankee Stadium and threw batting practice to the famed Babe Ruth, little did he imagine his career and life would take the turns that they did. One of the few players to ever go directly from college ball to the major leagues, Llewellyn made his professional debut with the legendary New York Yankees. His stay in the big league proved to be brief, however, and from there it was all downhill. Lew, as he was often called, dropped to the minor leagues and was eventually demoted, level by level, until he found himself playing for a semi-pro textile mill team in 1926. In essence, he worked his way down the baseball ladder, going the exact opposite direction of every other player with professional aspirations.

Though many people would have quit the game for good, Lew's lack

Hank Utley, a former star third baseman for North Carolina State University, is the co-author of the award-winning The Independent Carolina Baseball League, 1936–1938, *published by McFarland in 1999. A retired textile engineer, he makes his home in Concord, NC.*

Chris Holaday, a resident of Durham, NC, is the author of Professional Baseball in North Carolina: An Illustrated City-By-City History, *and co-author (with Marshall Adesman) of* The 25 Greatest Baseball Teams of the 20th Century Ranked.

of success as a player didn't deter him from dedicating most of his life to the game he loved. He eventually rose to prominence as a minor league administrator and league president. On April 2, 1948, during his second year as president of the Class B Tri-State League, Llewellyn told Smith Barrier, of the *Greensboro Daily News*, "If every boy broke into baseball with experiences as I had, I wonder how many would stay around for the second inning."

Born the son of a prominent attorney in the small town of Dobson, NC, in 1895, Llewellyn grew up playing baseball like most boys of that day. He soon discovered a talent for the game, and after high school he attended prep school at Oak Ridge Military Institute where he continued to play. In 1915 Lew earned an academic scholarship to attend the University of North Carolina in Chapel Hill.

At UNC, Llewellyn quickly established himself as an outstanding baseball pitcher (and hitter), as well as a budding leader. The United States entry into World War I interrupted Llewellyn's education, and he dropped out of school to work in a munitions plant in Virginia. Lew then joined the U.S. Navy, but the Armistice was signed before he saw any action. Lew returned to UNC in the fall of 1919, whereupon he decided to follow his father's footsteps into the field of law. He also made his return to the baseball diamond. As a pitcher he lost two games that spring, but would remain undefeated over the next two seasons. Lew finished his distinguished college baseball career with a record of 23–2, and in his senior year was responsible for 11 of his team's 17 victories.

Led by Llewellyn and first baseman Ernest "Mule" Shirley, who would later make the big leagues with Washington, UNC won the coveted state championship for three consecutive seasons—1920, 1921, and 1922. That type of college career brought many major league scouts calling, including those from the defending American League Champion New York Yankees. Lew jumped at a chance to play for such a great club and, according to contract records at the Baseball Hall of Fame, he received a bonus of $500 (a princely sum in 1922) for signing with the Yankees. His monthly salary was listed as $400. Immediately after the completion of his senior season, Lew reported to New York.

In 1948 Llewellyn recalled, "I was told to report direct to the New York office. I got off the train about seven o'clock in the morning, early in May 1922, and I got to the Yankee office before it opened. They told me to report for practice that day. I got out to the ballpark and they gave me a uniform. Right away they put me on the mound for batting practice, and I wasn't doing too badly when a big guy steps up on the left side of the plate. He's swinging a big bat and I know it's Babe Ruth. It was the

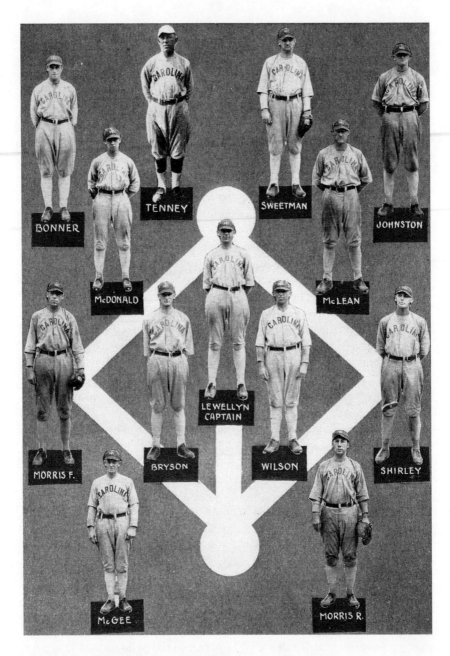

Llewellyn (center) with his 1921 University of North Carolina team. (Photograph courtesy of North Carolina Collection, University of North Carolina Library at Chapel Hill.)

first time I had ever seen him, and a knot comes up in my throat. I thought I would choke. I couldn't get the ball over the plate, three or four balls. Finally I got them in to him but I was scared to death.

"But I became Babe's favorite batting practice pitcher. I had good control, and I would send them right off the thigh on the inside corner. He used to hit four out of five pitches out of the ballpark. In the Polo Grounds he could knock them over the short right field corner with one hand. Babe would wait for my turn to pitch batting practice, or hurry to bat if I was about ready to quit. It was a grand experience for a rookie."

Manly Llewellyn, a big 6 feet, 4 inch, 195-pound rookie, made his major league debut on June 18, 1922. The Yankees were playing at Cleveland in a game that featured a match-up between Waite Hoyt and the Indians' Stan Coveleski, both of whom would go on to be enshrined in the Hall of Fame. While Coveleski pitched brilliantly, it was not a good outing for Hoyt. He gave up four runs in the first before manager Miller Huggins replaced him with George Murray, also a rookie from North Carolina. Murray fared little better than Hoyt had, allowing five more Indian runs, and Llewellyn got the call to pitch the eighth. In a one-inning stint he gave up no runs, one hit and no bases on balls. The Yankees lost the game 9–2 after failing to rally in the ninth.

On July 31, after he had several ribs broken by an errant throw during pre-game practice, Llewellyn was sent down to the Buffalo Bisons of the Class AA International League as part of the deal that brought catcher Benny Bengough to New York. Lew was finally recalled to the Yankees on September 12, but he never got into another game.

On January 30, 1923, Llewellyn was sold by the Yankees to the Atlanta Crackers of the Southern Association. Still troubled by the broken ribs, he appeared in only three games for Atlanta that season, wining none and losing two. At the end of the 1923 season Lew was dropped another level when he was sent to join the Greenville (SC) Spinners in the Class B South Atlantic League.

In 1924 Llewellyn finally played an entire season of professional baseball. In 31 games with Greenville he pitched 224 innings, gave up 247 hits and 125 runs. He finished the season with a 15–10 record, not bad considering the Spinners were a fourth place team that finished below .500.

On April 13, 1925, Llewellyn married Ruth Pitchford of Oxford, NC, and then returned to the Greenville Spinners. He won ten games that season and lost eleven as the Spinners continued their losing ways and dropped to sixth place with a record of 60–68. On Monday, July 13, 1925, the *Greenville News* reported: "Manly Llewellyn, the tall North Carolina lawyer who plays baseball in the summer for pleasure, seemed to hit his

stride in Knoxville Saturday, when he blanked the Smokies 2–0. He has pitched good ball all season but just at the wrong time, somebody would pole out a home run and take the game. In one game Lew allowed only four hits while the Spinners collected about ten but lost the game by a one run margin." On August 11 the *Greenville News* reported after a 3–1 loss: "Tar Heel lawyer allows seven hits and fans seven to take a bitter defeat."

After two losing seasons, the Greenville Spinners brought in well-known minor league player/manager Frank Walker to turn the team around in 1926. Walker proceeded to put together a talented team, and to do that some room had to be made on the roster. In what would be his only game with the Spinners that season, Llewellyn pitched well, giving up only three hits as the Spinners defeated the Columbia Comers 3–2 on May 2. Ten days later, however, his playing days in Greenville came to an end. An article in the newspaper reported: "Llewellyn Refuses to Be Shipped Away." The sub-heading stated: "Spinners Sell Him But He Balks on Reporting to Mississippi Club—Payless Suspension." Refusing to report to the Hattiesburg Pinetoppers of the Class D Cotton States League (the lowest level of professional baseball at that time), Llewellyn was released.

With a 30-year-old tired arm, Manly Llewellyn returned to North Carolina with his wife and looked for a place to locate his long delayed full-time law practice. Lew had been practicing law in the off-season in his hometown of Dobson since passing the North Carolina Bar exam in 1921, one year before reporting to the New York Yankees. He had actually failed to receive his degree from UNC in the spring of 1922 because he lacked a few academic hours. At that time, however, it was not unusual for lawyers to take the Bar exam without ever receiving a degree.

While continuing his search for a permanent home, word came to Llewellyn that a semi-pro team in the Cabarrus County, NC, textile mill town of Kannapolis was looking for players to help finish out the season. Eager to have an established player like Lew, the club offered good money he couldn't turn down. On August 14, the *Concord Tribune* reported that Manly Llewellyn, who had starred at UNC, debuted with the New York Yankees, and was recently released by the Greenville Spinners of the Sally League, was playing first base for the Kannapolis Towelers. Lew would hit .450 while playing seven games at that position.

When the 1926 season ended, Lew and his wife were living in a Kannapolis rooming house while considering making the town their new home. The baseball fans of nearby Concord had other ideas, however, and

Opposite: The 1926 Kannapolis team. Llewellyn, in the back row on the far right, is wearing his Greenville Spinners uniform. (Photograph courtesy of Hank Utley.)

started showing Llewellyn the advantages of establishing his law practice in the county seat instead of the unincorporated mill village of Kannapolis. So, in the fall of 1926, the Llewellyns decided to relocate seven miles to the south to Concord, NC.

In Concord, a new team was organized to represent the town in 1927, and club officers hired Lew as their manager. Though settling in to a full-time law practice, he was not ready to quit the game he loved. Textile mill baseball of that era was wild and uncontrolled, and the fans were rabid, but Llewellyn seemed to thrive in the atmosphere. Showing his skills as a leader, Lew guided his Concord Weavers team to the league's championship game in his first ever season as a manager.

The end of that season in Concord was dramatic. Lew's team was to meet arch-rival Kannapolis in the championship game, and tensions were high after rumors spread of fans ready to fight if their team lost. A reported 6,000 fans packed the ballpark for the showdown but, fortunately for Llewellyn and everyone else involved, the game was never played: a sudden torrential downpour just as it was getting underway sent everyone running for shelter, and the game was cancelled.

In 1928 Llewellyn decided to enter the world of local politics and ran for the office of Concord City Judge. He was elected and soon became well known for his sense of humor, as well as for his firm but judicious handling of the cases before him. Attesting to his popularity, Lew was easily re-elected at the end of every term. In 1940 he even made an unsuccessful bid for election as a State Senator, losing in a very tight race.

While serving as a judge, Llewellyn continued to play a prominent role in local baseball. He managed Concord's semi-pro team in 1928 and '29, and led the Weavers to great success both seasons. The 1929 team even produced two pitchers who would make the big leagues, Ray Prim and Buck Marrow. After the 1929 season Lew retired from the field, though for the next several seasons he would hold front office positions with the Concord club.

The fierce rivalries in the area's semi-pro league eventually led to high salaries being paid to attract quality players. Finally, a fully professional league, named the Carolina League, was formed for the 1936 season. Not a member of the National Association, the governing body for minor league baseball, the league was classified as "outlaw." Since they were ungoverned by the rules of the minor leagues, teams in this league were free to pay whatever salaries they could afford. Lured by what was often more money than they could make playing in the organized minor leagues, players came to the area from across the country to play in towns like Concord and Kannapolis. Judge Lew remained involved with Concord baseball while the town was in this league, serving as one of the team's directors.

During the winter of 1938–39, somewhat of a scandal hit the two-year-old Class D North Carolina State League. Apparently there were some rather large financial discrepancies in the league books, and team officials blamed the league president and essentially fired him. In search of a new leader to guide the league, the team leaders turned to a respected baseball man known for his integrity: Manly Llewellyn. Taking over for the 1939 season, Lew would guide the league for six seasons.

The N.C. State League was a rather compact league centered on the textile towns of the western Piedmont section of North Carolina. The distance between league towns was relatively short, so during Lew's presidency he made it his goal each season to see at least one inning of every game being played on Opening Night. Several of the league towns had fielded teams in the independent Carolina League, including Concord, which joined the N.C. State league after the outlaw loop disbanded following the 1938 season.

A lack of players, coupled with wartime restrictions, caused the N.C. State league to suspend operations after the 1942 season. Though professional baseball was gone in 1943, the unwavering support for the game by local fans led to the formation of a semi-pro league named the Carolina Victory League. Organized by Llewellyn, who served as its president, and other baseball leaders in the area, the league helped boost morale on the home front by providing a welcome distraction from the hardships of the war. Comprised of teams from several of the N.C. State League towns, the league consisted primarily of players who were either too young or too old for military service.

During the 1943 season, the manager and financial backer of the Salisbury club in the Victory League was found guilty of betting on his team's games. Even though this was semi-pro baseball, infractions of this kind were taken seriously, and league rules called for his immediate ouster from the league. Because of the party in question's position with his club, removal from the league would almost certainly bring about the end of the team. Many local fans were opposed to enforcing the rule, afraid it would kill the league as well, and leave them without baseball. As a testament to his integrity, Lew was completely willing to allow the demise of the league rather than to let the guilty party go unpunished. He suspected, however, that a team from nearby Mooresville would step in and fill the vacancy. Lew proved to be correct and the league continued play.

Anticipating the end of World War II, plans were made to resume play in the N.C. State League for the 1945 season. Llewellyn returned to his position as its leader and quickly got things up and running, a full season before every other league in the country that had suspended play. In

1946, baseball promoters from several cities in the Carolinas and Eastern Tennessee decided to form a new league. With franchises located in towns including Charlotte, NC, and Knoxville, TN, the Class B Tri-State League was formed. An experienced baseball man was needed to guide the fledgling league, and none better could be found than Manly Llewellyn.

Running two professional baseball leagues, in addition to practicing law and serving as a county judge, proved to be a huge undertaking, so after the 1946 season Lew decided to give up his job as president of the N.C. State League. Concentrating solely upon the Tri-State League, he oversaw its expansion into two new cities for the 1947 season. Under Llewellyn's guidance, the Tri-State League prospered and became very successful.

After the 1950 season, Llewellyn turned over the reigns of the Tri-State League and officially retired from baseball. Unofficially, however, he continued to exert considerable influence over area baseball affairs for many years. Probably one of the most experienced baseball men to be found anywhere, Lew's opinions on matters of the game were eagerly sought after. Never retiring from his other love, Llewellyn was still practicing law and presiding over the Cabarrus County Domestic Relations Court until his death in 1969.

Manly Llewellyn's chosen profession was the field of law, but his lifelong vocation was the field of baseball. Though a once-promising career as a major leaguer may not have turned out the way he would have preferred, Llewellyn was never discouraged by setbacks. As a player he at least got a taste of the big leagues, something thousands of minor leaguers fail to do. More importantly than his own personal achievements, however, Llewellyn's decisions and guidance helped shape the careers of countless players, umpires, and baseball executives. Using his contacts in the baseball world, Lew often went out of his way to help many young men secure college scholarships and sign professional contracts. Because of his commitment and his undying love for baseball, Manly Llewellyn left a lasting mark on the game and on the lives of people around him.

Llewellyn's professional record as a player:

Year	Team	G	IP	W	L	H	BB	SO	R	ERA
1922	New York	1	1	0	0	1	0	0	0	0.00
	Buffalo	16	86	6	6	111	44	78	58	6.07
1923	Atlanta	3	–	0	2	–	–	–	–	–
	Greenville	21	117	9	5	142	39	75	65	5.00
1924	Greenville	31	224	15	10	247	71	125	102	4.10
1925	Greenville	32	207	10	13	238	82	136	112	4.87
1926	Greenville	1	6.2	1	0	3	–	–	–	–

The Game
the Way It Ought to Be

by Marshall Adesman

It's easy to get angry with major league players. They make a lot of money—the base minimum is $200,000, and about half of them earn over $1 million annually—and only work half a year. They are pampered and spoiled and fawned over by everyone they meet, then turn around and act like spoiled, arrogant cusses; imagine that! And then, despite all these benefits, every few years they go out on strike as if they were dockworkers, depriving the Average Joe of flipping on the TV and watching a game after a hard day at work. Ungrateful bastards!

And, needless to say, it's a snap to get angry at major league owners and player agents, two groups who seem to be in a perpetual cage match in which they both walk away as winners. These paragons of capitalism are enough to make even the most rock-ribbed Republican long for a better economic system.

Because he couldn't hit the curve ball, Marshall Adesman moved from the outfield to the mound. Because the curve balls he threw from the mound were all landing in the outfield (and beyond), he then moved to the front office of several minor league franchises. He eventually retired from baseball altogether when the girls he kept trying to impress all thought he was a groundskeeper. He stays active, however, as a professional curmudgeon.

Nowadays it's also kind of easy to get angry with your local minor league team. Too many of them have become corporate, thinking only of the bottom line. My hometown Durham Bulls, glamorized by Hollywood in 1988, are no longer the sweet, small-time operation portrayed in *Bull Durham*; purchased by a large corporation at the beginning of the 1990s, they trot out unimaginative cookie-cutter promotions, then treat their fans disdainfully when they pour through the gates. The Frederick (MD) team of the Carolina League—the Class A Carolina League—charges $8 for general admission and $3.50 for a hot dog in a small ballpark that is somewhat less than state-of-the-art.

But before you throw up your hands and opt for arena football, let me tell you that all is not lost in Baseball Land. You can still experience the game the way it used to be, the way it ought to be. Just go to an Appalachian League town.

The Appy is the lowest rung of the minors, a place where major league teams send the high school kids (and some collegians) they draft every June. For most of these youngsters it is their first professional job, their first attempt to live the dream, and they get to do it in any one of ten small towns in the Tennessee, Virginia or West Virginia highlands, or (in one case) in the North Carolina piedmont.

The perfect place to start is Bluefield, West Virginia, where, except for the modern cars in the parking lot, you would swear you had been transported back to the Eisenhower years.

Bluefield is maybe my favorite place to watch a ballgame these days. General admission seating is just $2.50 per person, programs are $1.00. A representative from the Booster Club sits out front selling raffles for $1.00 apiece or three for $2.00; midway through the game, if you hold the lucky ticket number, you can split the pot with the Club.

Hamburgers sell for $1.50, same price as the nachos. A buck gets you a hot dog or a slice of pizza, and another $1.00 washes it down with a large drink (small cups are 50 cents). Peanuts, also, come in one-dollar and half-dollar designations, while popcorn, ice cream bars, gum and candy are all available for a couple of quarters.

The box seats are simple folding chairs found in any WalMart, and general admission seats are cement steps. No fancy cushioned chairs with backs and drink cups, just plain old cement steps, giving the place that Lincoln Memorial look. But this rusticity doesn't seem to faze anyone in the least. People bring lawn chairs, blankets, and seat cushions, settle into their usual spots and root for the home team, which has been, for more than 40 years, the first stop for most future Baltimore Orioles.

It is the place to meet. In the absence of a shopping mall, the old yard is frequently crawling with teenagers, most of whom pay little attention to the game. I know from personal experience that most minor league ballclubs have trouble drawing teens, so this is a welcome sight. And why not? They are out in the fresh air, easily seen so that they can't get into the kinds of predicaments teenagers often find themselves in, and they're spending money at the concession and souvenir stands rather than at less savory places.

Pulaski, Virginia, is not that far from Bluefield, but in order to get there you need negotiate a series of gut-wrenching S-curves along Interstate 81. Named for Casimir Pulaski, the 18th century soldier of fortune who helped the Thirteen Colonies escape from the shackles of Great Britain, Pulaski is a town of about 10,000 hearty souls, carved right into the granite of the Blue Ridge Mountains. Their facility, Calfee Park, was built in 1935 but does not have quite the same ambience as Bluefield's Bowen Field. But some years ago it offered up the perfect example of how to run a minor league operation.

In 1984 my personal baseball odyssey brought me to Durham, North Carolina, as Business Manager of the Bulls, then in the Carolina League. Miles Wolff, who owned the team at that time, was also responsible for two other clubs: independent Utica in the New York–Pennsylvania League, and Pulaski. Notice that I say "responsible for" rather than owned. The way the Appy League is set up, each club is legally owned by its major league affiliate, but the big club then signs a "management agreement" with someone who actually runs the franchise on a day-to-day basis. Miles had that arrangement with the Braves. As Business Manager, I was charged with overseeing financial affairs for all three teams operating under the Wolff umbrella.

In 1982, Miles' first year in charge, the team lost a couple thousand dollars, and the following year they only lost a few hundred dollars. It was Miles' opinion that this operation would always be small potatoes. Attendance was generally two or three hundred per night, and concession sales were marginal. I never fully understood why Miles agreed to operate this franchise, though I always suspected he did it as a favor to the Braves, who also supplied the players for his far-more-successful franchise in Durham.

My first task was to hire a General Manager, and for that I turned to an old Midwest League friend. Larry Avery had taken over in Burlington (Iowa) just weeks before I arrived in Waterloo, and he and I got to be pretty good buddies as we tried to turn a profit in a couple of small Iowa towns. When it came to running a franchise, Larry really knew his stuff, but he could be a bit abrasive at times and was known to rub a few people the wrong way, including advertisers and season-ticket holders, the

The grandstand at Burlington Athletic Park. (Photograph courtesy of Chris Holaday.)

kind of people you don't want against you in a power struggle. Which is apparently what eventually happened in Burlington, leaving Larry without a job. So I called him and told him he could come to Pulaski, but I also told him all the negatives, including the fact that this was definitely a one-year position. Without other viable baseball options, Larry took the job, figuring that if he did well it would help him land something better the next year.

A short-season circuit, the Appalachian League begins play around mid–June or so, which gives general managers only about 35 home games to plan for, about half the number Larry had dealt with back in Burlington. But rather than work at half-speed, he operated Pulaski as if it was a full-season club, aggressively seeking advertisers and sponsors for pro-

Opposite: Dreaming of big league stardom, the 1991 Burlington Indians. The odds of rookie league players making it all the way to the major leagues are very slim. One player on this team did make it, however. Outfielder Manny Ramirez, farthest left on the front row, is today one of the game's biggest stars.

motions. He purchased, out of his own pocket, a cordless phone, back when they were first becoming popular, because as a one-man staff he felt this was the best way to get things done around the ballpark and not miss any potentially important calls.

And the town responded. Attendance was up for the year, and when the season was over there was over $7,000 in the bank. Miles kept telling me to wait for the wave of bills that would show up and wipe out this surplus, but the only one that ever arrived was September's telephone charges, and they were consistent with what they had been all season long. Miles was so pleased that he sent Larry a $1,000 bonus check.

On the face of it, you would never think of a place like Pulaski as a good baseball town. It's small, in a generally poor location and features a less-than-ideal ballpark. Yet Larry Avery turned a $7,000 profit; how do you explain that? Simple: he worked hard and he worked it right, offering fun, family-oriented promotions almost every night. I guess you can "never judge a book by its cover."

Baseball's power brokers need to know that there are a lot of Pulaskis around the country, small towns that have little to distinguish them from innumerable other small towns. Why shouldn't they enjoy minor league baseball? In the current mood of profit maximization, why should only larger towns be granted franchises? Over the past several years we have seen the phenomenon of independent baseball, and while a few leagues have already come and gone, they have at least provided entertainment for tens of thousands of people in Pulaski-like hamlets.

Another good example is in Burlington, North Carolina. Situated about halfway between the much larger communities of Greensboro and Durham, Burlington sometimes struggles to maintain its own identity. But it offers a charming old-time ballpark with its own particularly unique history. In building a new yard for the 1960 season, the city purchased the grandstand from Danville, Virginia. Willie McCovey had played there just a few years before, but the team was now gone and the ballpark was sitting idle. Burlington spent $5,000 for the stands, shipped it the sixty or so miles piece by piece, and then re-assembled it on the site of their new park, which is now beginning its fifth decade.

Fans are close to the action in Burlington, and there is a constant hum in that grandstand, as something, like contests and music, is always going on—in addition to the game, of course. And the fans continue to turn out, well over 1,000 per game, possibly because they remember what it's like to be without the game. After drawing fewer than 300 people per night (on the average) in 1972 as a member of the full-season Carolina League, professional baseball left Burlington for fourteen years. Since gaining their

Appalachian League franchise in 1986, the fans have annually made their Indians one of the circuit's better draws.

These three towns all have a number of things in common, most especially the love they show for their teams. The fans do not take their baseball for granted, and neither do they ask for anything more, like a move up to a higher classification. A spot on minor league's lowest rung is just fine with them; they may only get 35 home games, but they make each one of them special. A far cry from New York or Los Angeles, it is truly the last bastion of old-time baseball.

The powers-that-be are not paying attention and that's a shame, because there are lessons to be learned. Baseball's leadership ought to be encouraging more towns to build ballparks and support a minor league team. Having a team might encourage more youngsters to play ball themselves, and might allow baseball to keep some of these young athletes who eventually gravitate to football and basketball.

This game—OUR GAME—is as much about Bluefield, Pulaski and Burlington as it is about Griffey, McGwire and Maddux. In fact, there are more Calfee Parks than there are Camden Yards. And there are (thank goodness!) more Larry Averys than Jerry Reinsdorfs. We may have every right to feel anger towards major league players, agents and owners, but not at The Game. The Game continues unabated in our hearts, and also on the playing fields of the Appalachian League.

A Remarkable Season

by Leverett T. Smith, Jr.

The year 1946 was a particularly happy year for the United States, for professional baseball, and for professional baseball in the city of Rocky Mount, North Carolina. World War II was over, the boys were coming home, the ballplayers were coming home, and interest in leisure activities, particularly in professional baseball, swept both the nation and the city.

But it is not easy to tell this from the newspapers of early 1946, for in Rocky Mount there was confusion even about the name of the team that was to play in the city. In mid–January an announcement appeared to the effect that Harry Soufas, a Wilson native who had starred for the 1942 Rocky Mount Rocks and then entered the armed services, had been named manager of the Rocky Mount team, which would play in the Class D Coastal Plain League, along with teams from New Bern, Fayetteville, Goldsboro, Kinston, Tarboro, Wilson, and Greenville. Soufas himself was back from active duty in Africa and Italy. The team would be called the "Bucs," a nickname frequently used by past Rocky Mount professional teams. As it turned out, the team that would win the 1946 Coastal

---

Leverett T. Smith, Jr., retired from North Carolina Wesleyan College in May of 2000 after 33 years of college teaching. He is the author of The American Dream and the National Game, *published in 1975 by the Popular Press of Bowling Green State University and now out of print.*

Plain League championship was named the Rocky Mount Rocks.

A few days later, sports fans learned that the team would be operated independently of any major league franchise. Frank Walker would be the president of the team, and, as the *Evening Telegram* put it, "backing the local laundryman in his venture are Avery Wynne, Rocky Mount radio station owner, Dr. Coyte Minges, H.A. 'Sandy' Easley, local tobacco man, and Ray Bandy, automobile dealer."

Walker, himself a former ballplayer and manager in Rocky Mount, began to gather together a group of hopefuls who, he hoped, would constitute a competitive team. Soufas would play as well as manage. Beyond that, Walker seemed worried. Late in February he was quoted as saying, "almost every former Buc he contacted had already made

Rocky Mount manager Harry Soufas. (Photograph courtesy of Harry Soufas.)

plans for a trip south with one of the major league clubs for training. However, Mike Drews, who held down the keystone sack for Rocky Mount last year indicated that he would be on hand for the season's opener." This, at least, was good news. Drews would be a key player in 1946.

There were stringent rules covering the sort of ballplayers one might carry on a Class D team. "According to league ruling," the *Evening Telegram* reported, "CPL teams are allowed three Classmen (players with more than three years' experience as pros), eight limited men (three years or less in the pro ranks) and four rookies." Soufas would be one of these classmen; before the season began, Walker would have two others, both of whom would play even more important roles in the team's success than Soufas. They were Charley Munday, a catcher who would lead the league in home runs (with 21) and the team in runs batted in (with 83), and Bill Kennedy, that year the league's most valuable player, a pitcher whose accomplishments with Rocky Mount in 1946 can compare to those of any pitcher in any league.

Meanwhile, Walker was trying out everyone in sight. Various articles in the *Evening Telegram* contained lists of those who signed contracts, and over fifty players performed at one time or another during the season for the Rocks. During spring training many more got their chance. One particularly poignant case that got some play in the *Telegram* was that of "Allan Morrison, outfielder, now attending Joe Stripps' Baseball School in Orlando." This notice appeared in late February, when readers also learned that Morrison originally "hails from Yakima, Washington." In April, an article reporting an exhibition game between the Rocks and the Durham Bulls, indicated that Morrison, a pitcher, was 40 years old, rather elderly for a baseball player. At this advanced age he was making "his first try at pro ball." And he had acquired the nickname "Grandpaw." The *Telegram* of April 18 even carried his picture. Alas, when the team roster was announced in the paper of 30 April, Morrison's name was not on it. "Grandpaw," along with many others less colorful, had been cut.

The team seemed an impressive one. The *Telegram* announced they were the best team in the league, "fast stepping and hard hitting." Sportswriter Bob Weirich called them "a scrappy bunch of little ballplayers." And they did, in fact, get off to a very fast start, holding a 5-game lead with a 21–6 record by the third of June.

Among the key players in this fast start were Drews, the second baseman, catcher Munday, manager–first baseman Soufas (who would spend most of the season playing third), and pitcher Kennedy, who already had a 7–1 record and had struck out 105 batters in just 67 innings. Three other players then on the team contributed largely to the success of the season. Outfielder Quentin "Pepper" Martin—who would also find himself catching, pitching, and playing third base before the season was over—played steadily in an outfield that was in a state of confusion all year. Melvin "Skeeter" Webb began and ended the season at shortstop, playing every inning of every game, providing, with Mike Drews, stability in the middle of the infield. The third player, Grover Fowler, Jr., known in the press as "Davey," may have been the most multi-talented member of the team.

At the end of the season he was named the league's best utility player, and it is hard to imagine a better one. At one point or another during the season, Davey played all three outfield positions, caught, pinch hit, played second and third base, and once even umpired a game. With all this, he managed to play in 100 of the team's 125 games, bat 361 times, lead the team in hitting with a .325 mark, hit 15 home runs, and finish second on the team to Munday with 68 runs batted in.

From this June 3 peak, the Rocks' fortunes described a deep parabola that touched rock bottom around the end of July when they found themselves some five games in back of the Wilson Tobs and with the press on their backs. They then began an ascent that continued until the season's end found the team with a 74–51 record, six games ahead of its closest pursuer.

On the eleventh of June, Bill Kennedy accomplished probably the most astonishing single feat of the season as he shut out the Goldsboro Goldbugs, 2–0. In the course of this game, Kennedy struck out 24 of the 27 men he retired. This gave him, according to the *Telegram*, 166 strike-outs in 87 innings. Kennedy had something of a personal duel going that year with Andy Tomasic, a strike-out pitcher for Kinston. Tomasic had struck out 22 in a ten inning game against Tarboro earlier in the year, but Kennedy outdid him, both in single-game achievements and over the year, as he went on to set what was then thought to be a single season record for strikeouts in professional baseball. The *Telegram* predicted that, "local fans will be talking about the tall southpaw for many years to come...."

Between the middle of June and early July the Rocks acquired four players who helped stabilize the team. On the thirteenth of June, third baseman Pete Hendershot quit the team to enter private business. He was replaced on the roster by Vince Colombo out of Atlantic Christian College in Wilson, who contributed a steady center field for the rest of the season. Five days later, Curt Balentine was signed to play first base and Harry Soufas took over third.

The other two additions were John Hanley, a pitcher-outfielder, and Herb Mays, an outfielder. Mays provided considerable offensive punch, hitting seven home runs and driving in 31 runs in the two months remaining in the season, then hitting five more home runs in the playoffs. Hanley, a versatile player, found himself pitching, pinch hitting, at third base, and in left and right field, all in his first week with the team.

In spite of these acquisitions, the team staggered through July, finding itself several games behind arch-rival Wilson by month's end. The *Evening Telegram* expressed considerable dissatisfaction with the team's play on several occasions. The first surfaced on June 25, the day after the Rocks sunk to a first place tie with Wilson, having been nipped by Kinston, 13–5. The *Telegram* reported that, "the loss was particularly disheartening to the Rocky Mount fans who have seen the locals quickly fade from a runaway, first place team with a five-game lead to an almost hopelessly lost aggregation. The team itself has seemed to have lost all color and interest during the last ten days in which they were able to win only two of nine games."

Newspaper grumbling continued in the issue of July 5, after the Rocks had dropped both ends of a doubleheader to Wilson: "Whether or not it was just the weather, the Rocks seem to have slipped back into their old 'I-don't-care' attitude. In the afternoon encounter in the municipal stadium they showed little of the 'hustle' necessary to win ball games, under any conditions."

While this sort of talk continued through the first three weeks in July, the Rocks continued to fall. On the eighth, the *Telegram* commented that, "the fight and hustle seems gone from the club. Even in winning they are without color and seem to be going through the motions of playing in a most listless manner … " Later in the month the paper began to resort to a sardonic humor in referring to the team. After a particularly humiliating loss, 18–9, to Tarboro, the paper remarked that the "Rocks" were "slowly ground to pebbles" during the course of the game. The next day, in response to a 15–12 loss in a game that featured 17 errors, in what may be a play on words, the paper summed up the situation in the headline "Locals Grovel."

This disenchantment with the team was accompanied by a growing irritation with the quality of the league's umpires. A note in a late June paper begins to tell the story: "Soufas, catcher Charley Munday, and Bill Kennedy were ejected from the game in the second inning, the former two by plate umpire Gibson for alleged arguing and the latter by base umpire and umpire-in-chief Pat Patterson." That the three most experienced players on the team, one of them the manager, were thrown out, seems significant, and though it is hard to make anything out of the phrase "alleged arguing," a certain animosity toward the umpire emerges.

Gibson's name appears often in newspaper diatribes against the umpiring. On the nineteenth of July, Rocky Mount was beaten at home by Wilson, 6–1, but this was not the main story in the *Telegram* the next day. The *Telegram* characterized the game as one "where fans forgot baseball and umpires needed police protection." Bob Weirich, in a separate column, lectured the fans on their bad behavior.

The next day, the *Telegram* was happy to report a "noticeable change in the umpires and the fans … with nary an argument to hold up the game and Clarence Roper and Thurman Britt working well and handling a nice game." The paper went on to single out Gibson for his villainy, saying "plate umpire Gibson, the cause behind most of the arbiter trouble in the loop, cut Soufas short Saturday night when, before the game, he warned him against argument of any sort. Most of the fines levied against Rocky Mount this season have been the doing of Gibson while the only times Soufas has been tossed from a contest have been at his hands."

Two days later, an event occurred that suggests the newspaper's reporting may have been just a bit partisan. It seems that Charley Munday had been suspended. The *Telegram* told the story this way: "Charley Munday, who was thrown out of Friday's game with Wilson by plate-umpire Gibson, has pulled down a three-game suspension and a $25 fine, though no one, including Munday, seems to know why." The fact that the league levied the fine and suspension suggests that Umpire Gibson may not have been quite so blind and arbitrary as the *Telegram* would have its readers believe. When Davey Fowler umpired a game in late August, it was because "the assigned arbiter appeared in a condition not conducive to good officiating." The *Telegram* praised Frank Walker for barring him from the field.

But as the Rocks righted themselves in late July and early August, the pennant race became the center of everyone's interest. For two weeks three teams—Wilson, Rocky Mount, and Kinston—stayed neck in neck. The seventh of August found them only eight percentage points apart. A week later the gap between the three teams had stretched to nine percentage points. The Rocks moved into first place on the twenty-third of August, and kept that position for the rest of the season, gradually lengthening their lead until it finally amounted to six games.

Throughout the last month, the newspaper's chief worry was over whether the Rocks' pitching staff was strong enough to carry them through. Aside from Bill Kennedy, they received very little consistent pitching. Kennedy, it happened, had as good a year as any pitcher is likely to have, finishing at 28–3 and winning his last seventeen games in a row. Nevertheless, it was reported, "a great deal of credit must go to other members of the mound staff who found themselves in the stretch drive when things were rough, John Hanley, Chuck Harrison, Al Kimmell and Jim Gudger with a final assist from Bobo Harrison."

Frank Walker and the other owners must have been happy too, for the attendance, which had been reported good all year, skyrocketed towards the end of the season and "had reached the 116,000 mark, probably a high for the circuit." The playoffs brought in many more fans. These the Rocks swept through, winning four out of five games from Goldsboro, then four out of six from Wilson. It was appropriate that Charley Munday should hit a three-run home run to decide the last game in the bottom of the tenth inning, for he had all year been a decisive offensive player. And it is also appropriate that Bill Kennedy should have been the pitcher of record, having pitched the top of the tenth in relief. It was Kennedy's fourth playoff victory to go with his 28 during the regular season. He struck out 47 in his 34 playoff innings, bringing his season's total to within two strikeouts of 500, a remarkable achievement. But then, for baseball fans in Rocky Mount, 1946 was a remarkable year.

And years later, the team's 1946 saga moved poet Arthur Mann Kaye to compose the following tribute to the team:

Minor League Baseball, Rocky Mount, 1946

> May was safe on an infield hit.
> Soufas sacrificed, but
> The throw to first was wild,
> And all the runners were safe.
>
> Martin sacrificed, runners advancing.
> Balentine grounded to Lingle and
> The latter man tossed late, trying
> To catch May at third, and
> All the runners were safe.
>
> Colombo walked to force in May.
> Fowler walked scoring Soufas as
> Mepler took over the mound. Kennedy
> Grounded to short, forcing Fowler
> At second while Balentine scored.
> The toss to first on a
> Double play try went wild and
> All the runners were safe.
>
> Webb homered down the left field line.
> Drews grounded out, second to first,
> To end the inning. Six runs, two hits,
> Two errors, none left.

Diary of a Minor League Season

by Miles Wolff

In 1980 I was awarded the franchise for the Durham Bulls of the Carolina League. The cost was $2,417. The ballpark was old and run down, and many doubted that minor league baseball could be successful in that city. Sometimes I think I was crazy for getting involved. I had been in and out of baseball for 10 years—mostly as a minor league general manager—and I figured I was ready to own a team. After all, I thought I knew more than the owners. Here is a diary of that first year. It was later published in *Inside Sports*.

April 8: It's 4 A.M. and I'm awake again. For the past two weeks I've been getting to bed at midnight or one o'clock and waking up four hours later, wandering around the apartment, thinking of what has to be done. Our home opener is a week away, and I have serious doubts that I'll live that long. That's what owning a minor league team does to you.

In October 1979, when the Carolina League awarded me the franchise,

After he sold the Bulls, Miles Wolff remained in baseball as president and publisher of Baseball America, which he sold in 2000. In 1993 he formed the Northern League, an independent minor league, and he is currently commissioner of that league.

it seemed like a good idea. Money was no problem. It never is when you don't have any. A few years back I'd applied for a franchise and had a big money man backing me. That deal fell through, and this time most of the directors thought I had the same partner. Who was I to tell them otherwise? I could scrape up the $2,500, which is the fee to the league. After I got the franchise I'd start hustling friends and family for the $30,000 worth of stock. I thought that would be enough to put me in good financial shape. It wasn't.

I haven't paid myself a salary in almost a month, and the team's bank account is close to zero. I had to pay the stadium rent up front (the city's no dummy). I've had expenses I never dreamed of ($50 to rent a machine to spray the infield green for the opener; the sod the city laid last fall is still brown—it's either dormant or dead). The advertisers are waiting until we open before they pay. Do they know something?

Minor league economics are simple. At least that's what I keep telling myself. I have a player-development contract (PDC) with the Atlanta Braves, which means they supply the players. In the last decade, with the major league clubs cutting back on their farm teams, PDCs have been hard to come by. However, the Braves are expanding their farm system this year. I'd worked for them in Savannah and Richmond, and that's one reason I got the Durham franchise.

Under the PDC, the Braves pay the salaries of the players, coaches and managers. They also fork out $5.50 of the $8.50 meal money, some of the hotel bills and assorted incidentals. It sounds like a good deal, and would be if the other expenses weren't so high. In the fall I had a projected budget of $100,000, but it may hit $150,000. Can we draw enough people to make that sort of money? Damn. I'll probably wake up at 3 a.m. tomorrow.

April 10: The season opens tomorrow in Winston-Salem, and our trainer, Gene Lane, has just discovered that our uniforms have been stolen. Aaauuuggghhh! Most of the home uniforms are gone, plus some equipment. Something about a ballpark attracts young vandals, and on every club I've worked with we've had problems with break-ins. But so soon? And they had to take our uniforms.

They were unique. One of our stockholders, Thom Mount, is with Universal Studios in Hollywood, and he'd gotten Marilyn Vance, the costume designer for the movie *Xanadu*, to make them. She'd come up with a special design made with a spandex fabric. It's been touch-and-go as to whether they'd be completed in time. They were just flown in yesterday. And, to use Mount's expression, they are "hot." They looked great when the team worked out last night.

I call Hank Aaron, the Braves' farm director, and he says Atlanta can send up an old set of its uniforms. We'll have to wear our old road uniforms at home. On the road, we'll have "Braves" on our shirts.

But what's really worrying me is I don't have any insurance for the loss. Marilyn says she can have more uniforms in six weeks, but I can't pay for them now, so we'd better draw some crowds before the new uniforms arrive or I'll have to start "the-check's-in-the-mail" routine.

April 13: We're 0–2, and manager "Dirty" Al Gallagher is in the office, bitching because the game was rained out in Winston-Salem and we didn't ever call in time to keep the team from making the 170-mile round trip. The bus turned around as soon as it got there. Pete Bock, my general manager, assures Dirty Al it won't happen again.

I've heard Al's a little difficult to deal with. I don't think so. He cares about winning, and he cares about his players—qualities often lacking in minor league managers. But most important, he's a Clint Courtney man. Everybody in baseball has their own story about "Scrap Iron" Courtney, a squat, bespectacled catcher who was known to like a beer now and then. After his playing career, Scraps was a pretty good minor league manager, and I had the good fortune to have him for a few years in Savannah. Al had him a year-and-a-half in Richmond before Courtney died of a heart attack at 48. Scraps was a big influence on both of us, and anybody who loves him is OK in my book.

Hiring Bock as general manager may be my luckiest move. Pete is 29, and he wants responsibility. For the last three years he's been an umpire. Working in the minors at any job is tough, but being a minor league umpire is the toughest. Last season Pete was in the Carolina League after having worked in the Western Carolinas and the Appalachian Leagues.

Umpires' pay in the Carolina League is the highest in all Class A leagues, but that's not saying much. Umps make $1,100.00 a month for the four-and-a-half month season, but out of this, they have to pay all meal and motel costs. Since they're always on the road (140 games), it's a near miracle if they break even.

Pete was a good umpire, but he was looking at five or six more years in the minors. Even then there would be no guarantee he would get a shot at the big leagues. More important, he is married with an eight-year-old son, and the thought of being away from them so much was getting to him. However, he wanted to stay in the game, and he approached me for the front-office job.

There is no set way to get a job in a minor league front office. At the baseball winter meetings there'll be dozens of job applicants hanging

around the lobby with briefcases full of résumés. Many don't have a clue as to what the minors are about. Some come from sports administration graduate school programs, where they teach press releases and public relations. They aren't prepared for cleaning the restrooms when the weekend cleanup man gets drunk, or pulling out the tarps in the mud in your good shoes because the grounds crew consists of one.

Umpires in the minors know the score, and they aren't jock sniffers. Some of the job seekers just want to be around ballplayers. Pete has paid some dues and is willing to pay some more to get in the front office. His salary is $700 a month, plus 10 percent of his preseason ticket and advertising sales. If things get better financially, he'll get a raise.

April 15: It's the sixth inning and half the lights on the field are out, the water is no longer running in the bathrooms, and I'm laughing. Normally, I wouldn't be amused. Normally, I'd be panicking. Except Pete is doing the running around now. It's a relief to see someone else sweating.

It's our home opener, and if Murphy's Law was ever written for a specific venture, it was for minor league openers. Everything *always* goes wrong on Opening Night. How were we to know that the wrong circuit breakers were installed when they added lights to the field? Or that the city laid the wrong size water pipe to feed the stadium? But that's Pete's responsibility, so I can sit and snicker.

Also, I feel good. We've drawn 4,418 fans, the money's counted, the opening-pitch ceremonies only went 10 minutes past schedule, and we're operating (if Pete ever gets the lights back on).

At 5 P.M. today I wasn't sure if we were going to be operating. That's when the health department man showed up. He'd come two weeks earlier and placed so many restrictions on our concession stand that I was thinking of saying "the hell with it." He wanted us to get our own ice-making machine, among other things, and install a new ceiling. Needless to say, we didn't have the money. But the city of Durham crews helped us out. At 5:30 tonight the health man said we could open our concessions.

Opposite: The 1980 Durham Bulls. *Front:* Blane McDonald, Albert Hall, Gene Lane (trainer), Gerald Perry, Milt Thompson. *Row 2:* Rick Coatney, Andres Forbes, Paul Runge, Steve Steib, Tommy Thompson, Jeff Matthews, Gary Reiter. *Row 3:* Pete Bock (general manager), Al Gallagher (manager), Dave Slade (play-by-play), Gil Ryan, Glen Bockman, Russ Kerdolf, Mike Smith, Rick Behenna, Pete Texeira, Juan Alduay, Bob Veale (coach), Miles Wolff (president). *Row 4:* Ike Pettaway, Dom Chiti, Al Pratt, Alvin Moore, Ronnie Rudd. (Photograph courtesy of Miles Wolff.)

What a relief. He still wants us to do some things, but we've been selling hot dogs and Coke and a lot of beer, even though the temperature is 45 degrees. It's going to be a good concession night, and we should gross close to $4,000.

The lights have come back on. It looks like we'll finish the game.

April 18: We're clicking. After Opening Night, our attendance was 642 and 884, but both were good money crowds, particularly considering the temperature was around 40 degrees. Tonight we've got 2,316, and the crowd is exceptionally lively. It doesn't hurt that we're winning, but I've never seen such enthusiastic minor league fans. We've got some Duke students who chant "Let's Go Bulls!" and everybody is picking it up.

I've been walking around outside the stadium trying to see where people are parking. Durham Athletic Park is an antique, and, unfortunately, there is parking for only 80 cars. After that, people have to park on the streets. The ballpark was built in the 1930s, and it's in a downtown warehouse district. Right field is only 291 down the line and 340 in the power alleys, and that's because we've got this big warehouse directly behind the fence. The park is intimate, with the 5,000 seats right on top of the players. The fans can see and hear everything.

April 19: Am I crazy? I can't believe we're doing this. Pete and I are in the parking lot, yelling our heads off, asking people *not* to come into the park. You don't do that in the minors. Usually, you've got to beat people over the head or kidnap them to bring them in. But tonight, incredibly, we don't have any more room. Every seat is taken, people are standing everywhere, and the line to buy tickets is the length of the parking lot.

Okay, it's Jacket Night, which is a decent promotion, with every kid 14 and under getting a free jacket. But I've had giveaways before, and you are usually lucky if you draw an extra 500 to 1,000 people. We were looking for around 3,000 fans tonight, but the jackets were gone a half-hour before game time. We're giving out special rainchecks so kids will get a jacket when we order more.

The best part is that these are paying fans. In the minors, there is a tendency to put out free tickets or do some other mathematical wizardry, where every person is counted two-and-a-half times. But we've got 5,791 people tonight. And they like us. On some nights when I've had big promotion crowds, the fans would just sit on their hands, waiting for the seventh inning so they could have an excuse to leave. These fans are staying, and they're having a good time, and they're chanting "Let's Go Bulls" in unison. It's almost like the big leagues. Hell, I might as well join in. Let's Go Bulls!

May 10: I've learned something about Pete Bock that sounds like it's out of *The Twilight Zone*. His grandfather is buried on the pitching mound. No kidding. His grandfather was a minor league pitcher name Claude "Buck" Weaver who won 18 games for Durham in 1946. He started in the minors in 1928 and was a professional pitcher until he was almost 50. When he died in 1967, his body was cremated and his ashes were raked into the mound at Durham Athletic Park. Now his grandson is general manager here. Weird.

May 13: It's been quite a first month. We've been successful beyond my wildest hopes. The team is in first place and at one point won 12 straight. Dirty Al has the team stealing bases at every opportunity, and the running is intimidating other teams.

The crowds are still averaging better than 2,000 per game. An important reason is beer. This is the first time it's been legal to sell beer at the stadium. North Carolina is fairly regressive when it comes to beer and liquor laws, and the college crowd has taken to coming to the games. It's a happy crowd, and we've yet to have the first incident. One newspaper headlined us as "The Best Bar in Town." Of course, Durham isn't exactly a great bar city.

I like the overall mix of our fans. With a lot of minor league clubs, the crowds were usually a combination of over-50s and under-14s. But it seems like we've got every age and group coming to see the Bulls: college, blue-collar, businessmen, blacks, women, and kids. We've even got a blind fellow who comes with a friend, and he boos the umpires with the rest of the fans.

Tonight there was a performance that had the fans laughing. We won 6–3, but the theatrics of Buddy Hunter, the Winston-Salem manager, overshadowed the game. Last night a Winston-Salem player hit a home run over our short right field wall. But the ball bounced against a scoreboard and came back on the field. The umpire didn't see that it had gone over the fence and ruled the ball in play, leaving the player with only a triple. Hunter argued and lost.

Tonight the same umpire called another one against his team. Hunter argued and was ejected. Then the fun started. He grabbed a ball from the dugout and ran to the right field where he threw the ball against the fence and, mocking the umpire, signaled "home run." Then he flipped a coin and signaled "ball in play." After running around a bit more he sat on first base and started taking off his shoes. Pretending they were hand grenades, he bit the ends and lobbed one shoe at each umpire. Still in his stocking feet, he sprinted to the clubhouse as both teams and the fans gave him a standing ovation. Even the umpires were laughing about the incident. Damn if I don't love the minor leagues.

June 10: The newspapers are getting on the team. A column in today's paper is headlined "June Swoon," and it goes on at length about the Bulls' slump. The team's nine-and-a-half-game lead has dwindled to three, and the play has been lackluster. No way I can fault the newspapers.

One of my main worries in taking over the Durham franchise was how the media would react to the club. This is ACC territory, and with Duke, the University of North Carolina and North Carolina State all within a 25-mile radius, I thought a minor league team might take a back seat. The Durham press, however, has treated us like any other important sporting event in the area.

The problem is what to do about the team. There is not much a minor league operator can do about the players. We're dependent on the Braves, and since they pay the salaries, I can't complain. And there is not much to complain about. They've given us an excellent team, and Dirty Al is confident it's only a mild slump.

One reason for the slump is the call-up of one of our top players. It's a fact of life in the minors that if someone is going good, you'll probably lose him. On May 29 Atlanta moved our second baseman, Jeff Matthews, to the Class AA club in Savannah. Jeff was hitting .341, and when a Savannah infielder was injured, he was the natural player to go. But Jeff is something of a sparkplug and his departure has hurt us.

Jeff is 23 years old and this is his fourth year of pro ball. The Braves don't consider him much of a prospect, and he has been one of those utility infield types that an organization can put on any club. He'll play well and help the better prospects develop. He'd been sent here as a backup second baseman, but early on he got in the lineup and has been going great. In the first week of the season a group of fans formed a Jeff Matthews fan club and carried signs with his number 17 around the park. He had been a clutch player. That's why it's so tough to lose him.

I believe playing in front of responsive and large crowds helps players. Albert Hall is a quiet young man who hadn't distinguished himself in his three previous seasons. He was erratic fielding shortstop, but he's adjusted to a change to left field and is hitting better than .300. Already he's stolen 43 bases in 54 attempts, and when he gets on base, the park comes alive. The fans start chanting *"Al-bert, Al-bert,"* and it pumps him up. It also tends to unnerve the opposition, and his speed is the talk of the league.

June 22: The first half ended three nights ago and we won the pennant in the North Carolina Division. After out slump earlier in the month, the team bounced back. When we swept Kinston, we clinched first place. We drew more than 81,000 in the first half, a figure I would have been happy with for a season's attendance.

Promotions have been important in our attendance. We have something going on almost every night. We've had 10-cent hotdog night, Max Patkin (the baseball clown), free peanuts, wristband night, employees group night, and anything else we could do to attract the people.

Our game was on TV this afternoon, and you can probably count on one hand the number of minor league teams that have any of their games televised live. Normally, we play at night, but when the local CBS affiliate wanted to televise, we switched. There were five cameras around the park, and it was a good production. The park looked great: the centerfield camera, taking a wide-angle shot, made the old stadium look big league. We had a crowd of 2,851, but most of the staff was in my office peering at a small portable color set.

It was a good game for TV. We lost, but there was a grand slam, great catches, and five stolen bases. But the real show was Al Gallagher. To begin with, he hadn't wanted to get thrown out. He's enough of a ham that he intended to be on TV all nine innings. And he's past the stage of his career when he gets ejected for show.

But in the seventh inning he argued over a close play. It was only a mild argument, but he sprayed some snuff on the umpire and was ejected. That's when Al explained that the snuff spray was accidental. But it was too late. Then Al decided he might as well get his money's worth. He yelled for maybe three minutes, running from one umpire to the other, and then he charged home plate and started reaching in his cheek. And with the TV cameras focused close up, he pulled out this wet, brown, sloppy chew and threw it in the center of the plate. *Splat!* With the cheers of the fans echoing all over the park, he marched to the clubhouse. Great family entertainment.

July 1: I've spent the day in Rocky Mount, North Carolina, with league president Jim Mills, Winston-Salem owner Ervin Oakley and Kinston general manager Ray Kuhlman. We've got a mess on our hands. The Rocky Mount Pines are about to fold. Today is payday, and there isn't enough money to cover the players' checks. The team may not take the field tonight. The owner lives in Florida and apparently is refusing to send any more money. It's a complicated situation that keeps getting worse.

To begin with, there was no major league working agreement. The owner, who runs baseball camps along the East Coast, wasn't at the annual league meeting (he has never come to any meetings), but his manager, Mal Fichman, told the league that a working agreement wouldn't be a problem. The league directors were assured that the club would be competitive and some players would be loaned from major league organizations. While the situation didn't appear promising, the league needed an eighth city, and here was someone willing to come in without a major league working agreement. So Rocky Mount got its franchise.

A seven-team league makes no sense at all. The major leagues want their players playing every night, and with an odd number of teams there would be three and four days in a row that a team wouldn't play. This messes up pitching rotations and a team's competitive edge. A minor league operator would lose 10 home dates. This could mean the difference between profit and loss.

The first Rocky Mount general manager had no baseball experience and got off to a late start selling ads. When the season began there was little pre-season income, a necessity if you hope to break even. He quit in the first week of the season, and since then they've been through two other GMs. The team has been horrendous, with a 14–55 record in the first half and a crowd average of about 300. The ownership had hoped to make money by opening a baseball school in Rocky Mount and drawing campers because of the association with the team, but the school has been a dud.

We've been meeting with Fichman most of the day and talking to the owner by phone, trying to work out a solution. Mal is a long-time minor league GM, but he has little experience on the field. Quite a few people wonder what Mal is doing as manager, but I think I know. Being a minor league GM is a dead end if you want to advance in the administrative side of the big leagues. Only rarely will a minor league GM be hired for an assistant farm director job (the only one that leads anywhere in the big leagues); mostly former players or scouts are hires. Minor leaguers can get jobs in the sales and promotions side, but they're generally flunky positions. If you have big league aspirations, being a minor league GM can be frustrating. Mal is trying to prove he can be competent in the player and administrative side.

The tragedy in all this is the players. These are guys who want to play baseball, and you got to want to play when your salary is $325 a month. The average on other teams is in the $800 to $900 range. But Rocky Mount has mostly players who've been released by major league organizations, and this is their last chance at continuing their playing careers.

By the end of the day we've reached a temporary solution. The league is going to lend the Pines $2,000 to meet expenses; I'm going to guarantee them $1,000 for each series in Durham; and Ervin Oakley will pay motel bills for the trips to Winston-Salem. Some other clubs aren't going to be happy with the loan from the league. Both Kinston and Alexandria operated as independents in 1978. They lost $105,000 between them but they paid all their bills without asking for help.

There is still no guarantee that Rocky Mount can last the season. But Durham has six more home dates with the team, and I'll probably lose 15,000 in attendance if they don't make it. I sure hope they last.

August 1: Our secretary quit. She was excellent—a tremendous personality—but a lack of communications led to an unfortunate situation. She and her husband had become friendly with a player and his wife. It's not always advisable for the front office to get too close to the players, because often you're working for different ends. But it's hard to tell someone who their friends can be. The player started spouting off in the clubhouse on some player movements he shouldn't have known about. Dirty Al asked me to remind our secretary that anything she knew about should be kept in the office. Unfortunately, she took it personally and quit.

When she left, she listed a number of grievances, and one was simply that the job wasn't fun anymore. I could have told her that in April. July and August are never fun. It's difficult to describe how mentally and physically fatigued you can be at the end of the season. Since early March, when the crunch started, it's total involvement and immersion in baseball. Once the season starts, game days run on a 9 A.M.–midnight schedule. When the team goes on the road, you still put in an eight to 10 hour day.

At first, it is exhilarating to be so involved, to know that every night you're working against a deadline; everything has to be ready to seat, feed, and take care of 2,000 people, while putting on a show with a cast of 50. By June, though, the weariness sets in, and by August you go through the motions, hoping for September.

This year has been even worse because of the intense heat. We've had games end at 10:30 and, with no cooling nighttime breezes, I'll be sweating like it's high noon. Everyone is getting on everyone else nerves, and it's not easy to be pleasant to someone with a complaint you don't want to handle.

It's just as bad for the players. The 140-game schedule includes only three off-days all season. That's seven days a week of baseball, with 300-mile bus trips, strange motels and $8.50 a day on the road for meal money. One year I did play-by-play broadcasting in the International League and traveled with the team. Since then, I've never made the often-heard comment about players having it easy, never having to go to work until 4 p.m., getting to sleep all day and watch the soaps. It ain't that way. It's tough.

The big leagues want it that way—tough. The majors have a few more off-days, but theirs is a 162-game schedule, and they need to know how prospects respond to the grind. It's easy to be a phenom in early May, but the test is August. If a player is still playing with intensity and is managing to keep his average up, maybe he'll have a shot at making it.

August 29: The game ended 10 minutes ago, but 3,000 people are still here, cheering their heads off. I'm sitting in the stands myself, just watching. We've done it. This is the first time it's hit me. Sometimes I get so caught up in the day-to-day worries it's hard to see what's happening. We've drawn more than 170,000 fans—double what I'd hoped for—and we should recoup our original investment and maybe make $15,000 more.

Tonight's game didn't mean anything, since we clinched the pennant last night. And we were playing Rocky Mount. They'd managed to limp through the season, bills and all, but their record is 24–112. Still, tonight 3,000 people showed up. Rick Behenna, who's been erratic all season, pitched a no-hitter, and Albert Hall stole his 100th base. The fans were into this game as if it were the seventh game of the World Series: they were cheering and yelling and loving every minute. Now they're screaming as Behenna takes another bow, and there goes shy Albert sliding into second with the game long over.

Durham loves this team. You can go through a minor league career and never see that. The Durham Bulls are an important part of the community. Little kids wear out T-shirts, grown men walk around town with our caps, and girls fall all over our players. I keep saying to myself that this is the minors, that it can't happen like this. I wish I could take tonight home in a bottle and nip on it all winter long. Hell, maybe I can.

Postcript: My ownership of the Bulls continued until 1991. In the 1980s attendance continued to rise, and the franchise became one of the most successful in all of minor league baseball. In 1987 the movie *Bull Durham* was made, which catapulted the team to national prominence. Pete Bock was GM for the first two years of the Bulls. He left to become GM of the Hawaii Islanders of the Class AAA Pacific Coast League. He returned to Durham in 1987 and served as the baseball advisor during the filming of

Bull Durham. Later he became GM of the Raleigh IceCaps minor league hockey team. He is currently president of the Coastal Plain League, a summer college baseball circuit that fields teams in both Carolinas and Virginia. Al Gallagher continued as a minor league manager until 1985. He then changed careers to become a sixth grade elementary school teacher in Clovis, California. He couldn't stay away from baseball, however, and in 1995 he returned to the game. Al is currently managing in the Northern League. Several members of the 1980 Bulls went on to appear in the big leagues, including Albert Hall, who spent parts of nine seasons in the majors. His best year was 1987 when he hit .284 and stole 33 bases in 92 games for the Braves.

A Special Doubleheader — July 4, 1911

by Parker Chesson

In the early 1900s, the Fourth of July was a festive day all across America. Baseball games were an important part of a full slate of outside activities, which ran from early in the morning until the early evening hours. This was certainly the case on July 4, 1911, in Elizabeth City, North Carolina. The Elizabeth City nine, as writers often called baseball teams in those years, played a doubleheader against the Suffolk Nancies. The Elizabeth City Tar Heels and five other semi-pro teams from Southeastern Virginia, including Suffolk, comprised the Tidewater League.

During the first half of the twentieth century it was common for a baseball team to play a doubleheader with a nearby team on the Fourth of July. Usually the first game was played in one town in the morning and the second game in the other town in the afternoon. On this day in 1911, the first game between Elizabeth City and Suffolk was played in Suffolk. The challenge in those days, particularly in Northeastern North Carolina, was trying to travel over very poor roads, since paved roads were

Parker Chesson is currently writing a book on the history of baseball in Northeastern North Carolina, with a particular emphasis on the Albemarle League. That league was one of the top semi-pro leagues in the country in the years shortly after World War II.

practically nonexistence in rural parts of the state. Norfolk Southern Railroad completed the first railroad connection from Norfolk to Elizabeth City in 1881. About 1910, a connecting line was built between Elizabeth City and Suffolk, passing along the western edge of the Great Dismal Swamp. Though there is not a record of the route they used that day, the July 4, 1911, train probably used this railroad in making the Elizabeth City to Suffolk trip.

Early on that Fourth of July morning the Elizabeth City Tar Heels team and a large number of fans crowded the depot's loading platform at the end of West Main Street. The first game of the doubleheader was to start in Suffolk at 10:30 a.m. The second game would be back in Elizabeth City at 4:30 p.m. The train left at 7:30 a.m., carrying the Tar Heels and their fans, traveling westward and then to the north towards Suffolk on its nearly two-hour trip.

In the prior week's issue of *The Weekly Advance*, a front-page article promoted the games between the Tar Heels and the "Nancies of Goober City," a reference to the importance of peanuts, or goobers, in the Suffolk economy. Round-trip fare for the excursion was one dollar. The newspaper stated that, "The excursionists will pass through a part of the historic Dismal Swamp, which of itself should be very interesting to many people in Elizabeth City who have lived here for years within a few miles of the great swamp and have never seen it."

The Tidewater League had opened its season in April. On April 21 the Tar Heels began their season in Elizabeth City with a 13–3 win over Suffolk before about 1,500 fans. The league's teams had played over 60 games by the Fourth of July. Elizabeth City was in first place, easily outdistancing the other five teams.

Other than several newspaper articles, a few of them with box scores, little is known about the players or details of the games. Some of the articles emphasized the outstanding talents of two college players who had joined the Elizabeth City team in early June.

Dave Robertson, 6'0" and 185 lbs., was a native of Portsmouth, Virginia, and a four-sport star at North Carolina A & M College (now North Carolina State University), starring in football, basketball, baseball, and track. Edgar Bundy was a star athlete at Trinity College (now Duke University). Both Robertson and Bundy traveled to Elizabeth City after their spring terms ended. One newspaper account tells about them traveling by train through the night, arriving in Elizabeth City early one morning, and being pressed into action that afternoon. Robertson, who threw left-handed and hit from the left side of the plate, could play almost any position. Bundy, smaller than Robertson, was fleet of foot and a good hitting

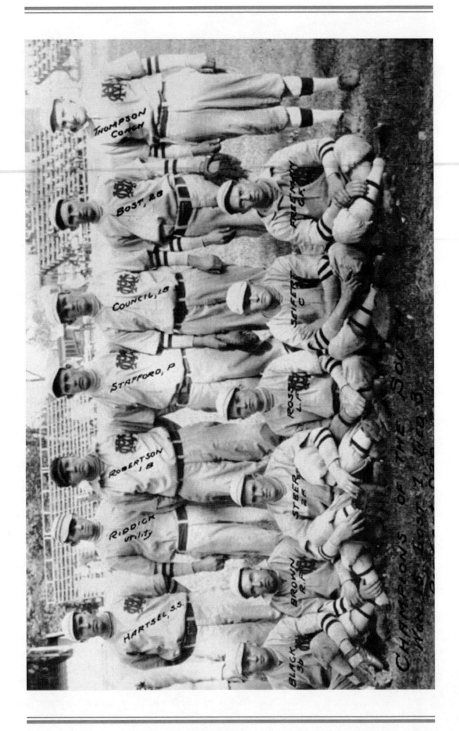

CHAMPIONS OF THE SOU...
Won by Bost, 1 Tip 3...

THOMPSON
COACH

BOST, 2B

COUNCIL, 1B

STAFFORD, P

ROBERTSON
1B

RIDDICK
utility

HARTSEL, S.S.

FREEMAN
C.F.

SEIFERT
C

ROSS
L.F.

STEER
2B

BROWN
R.F.

BLACK
3B

infielder. Both of them were with the Elizabeth City entourage during its early morning Fourth of July trip to Suffolk.

Little is known about the details of the two games played that day, except that Elizabeth City won both ends of the doubleheader. After the morning game in Suffolk, the Nancies and their fans loaded up with the Elizabeth City folks and left for Elizabeth City at 1:30 p.m. The second game of the day started at 4:30 p.m. One can easily visualize the scene on the train that day. Baseball players, probably in uniform, mingled with fans and had a good time on both legs of the trip. Undoubtedly, picnic food was in abundance, since there was little time to waste between the two games.

Dave Robertson was a hero in Elizabeth City that summer and was remembered by the local folks for many years. He went back to North Carolina A & M College that fall and played college ball in 1912. John McGraw, legendary manager of the New York Giants, then signed Robertson, and he played his first game for the Giants on June 12, 1912. He went on to play nine years in the majors, seven under McGraw, and compiled a lifetime batting average of .287. He hit .300 or higher in 1916, 1920, and 1921. In 1916 and 1917 Robertson led or tied for the National League lead in homers—with 12 each year. Obviously, this was in the dead ball era.

Robertson also compiled another notable record during the 1917 World Series with the Chicago White Sox. Though his team lost in six games, he was the star of the Series. He set a Series record by collecting 11 hits in 22 at bats. This record would stand for the next 36 years, until Billy Martin broke it with 12 hits in the 1953 six-game World Series between the Yankees and the Dodgers.

Years later, Robertson loved to tell a story about John McGraw. In a 1915 game with the Cubs at the Polo Grounds, the Giants had a man on base and McGraw signaled him to bunt. A fat pitch came in and Robertson hit it into the right-field bleachers and won the game, 3–2. Robertson reported, "I pranced to our dugout expecting to be praised for my game-winning feat. What happened? Why, McGraw fined me $500 for disobeying orders."

After his major league career ended, Robertson managed Richmond and Norfolk in the old Virginia League in the 1920s. He later worked as a game warden for the Commonwealth of Virginia for 28 years. Born September 25, 1889, he died November 5, 1970.

The 1910 North Carolina A & M College baseball team. Dave Robertson is in the back row, fourth from left. (Photograph courtesy of the University Archives, North Carolina State University Libraries.)

Edgar Bundy, the other star Tar Heels player that summer, graduated from Trinity College and had a long career in public education. He returned to Northeastern North Carolina in the late 1920s to serve as superintendent of the Perquimans County public schools, and later headed the Elizabeth City public school system. While in these positions, Bundy was a strong supporter of organized baseball. In 1930, while in Perquimans County, he helped organize the Albemarle League, a fast semipro league that played off-and-on until the late 1950s.

The Fourth of July games marked the halfway point for the Tidewater League. The July 7, 1911, issue of *The Weekly Advance* noted that Elizabeth City was declared the pennant winner with a record of 44–23, well ahead of second place Norfolk. Then the league collapsed. A few games were played in the second half of the season, but then play abruptly stopped. Though the record has little factual information, it appears the teams had severe financial problems and simply stopped playing.

Baseball remained popular and continued to be played in the small towns of rural Northeastern North Carolina, but it would be nearly twenty years before the Albemarle League, another strong semi-pro league, was organized.

Triangle Baseball—
A Hollywood Epic

by Marshall Adesman

Yes, sir, thank you very much, sir, I appreciate your granting me a few minutes of your valuable time to pitch my idea. No, sir, I've never been inside a Hollywood studio before; I guess I am a little nervous.

But this is such a good story, full of drama and intrigue and warmth and even irony, with heroes and villains and hard-working people, the kind of story I just know the American public will take to right...what's that? Well, sure, I guess I could include a sex scene.

May I give you a little background first? Thank you. The story is set in North Carolina, and once upon a time the Tar Heel State was kind of a sleepy place, fueled by tobacco and textiles. But there was baseball everywhere, from the mountains to the coast, in big cities and little burgs. In fact, in 1948, 48 communities were represented in Organized Ball before things began to change in America. The clothing industry moved to

Marshall Adesman is a former minor league baseball executive who has worked for both the Durham Bulls and the Carolina Mudcats. Before ending up in North Carolina his career in baseball took him to such far-ranging places as St. Petersburg, FL, Amarillo, TX, and Waterloo, IA. Co-author of The 25 Greatest Baseball Teams of the 20th Century Ranked, *published by McFarland in 2000, Adesman is currently employed by Duke University.*

different countries, and the Surgeon General started tobacco on a down-
ward spiral. Air conditioning and television kept people indoors, and when
they ventured out they could ride in their now-affordable automobiles on
new interstate highways, allowing them to see parts of the country they
had only read about in magazines. In 1957, just six North Carolina towns
were still found on the baseball landscape.

There had been teams in both Raleigh and Durham since the earli-
est years of the 20th Century, but by the late 1960s poor attendance in both
towns forced them to merge and field just one team, with home games in
both towns. That shotgun marriage lasted just four summers, and when
play concluded after the 1971 season so did the life of the Raleigh-Durham
Triangles.

Baseball returned to Durham in 1980, and by then North Carolina
was a much different state. While two tobacco plants still operated in
town, the computer industry and related high-tech businesses had become
important economic cogs, bringing with them young employees with a
good deal of disposable cash. In their first year back in the Carolina League,
the Durham Bulls drew almost 176,000 fans, a franchise record and league
high. By 1985 they were setting the attendance standard for all of Class A,
and by 1990 they were out-drawing all Double-A teams and a dozen
Triple-A franchises.

And they were doing this in old Durham Athletic Park, a 5,000-seat
facility built in 1939. The old girl was still quite the charmer, all right, but
she creaked under the weight of some 4800 fannies per night. A new ballpark was needed to keep up with the burgeoning demand, which was not
just a Durham phenomenon. There were success stories all over the minor
league map, literally from Maine to California, and others wanted their
share of the pie. That included the Raleigh area, without a team for nearly
twenty years. Baseball rules prohibited locating two franchises within 35
miles of one another, which eliminated the city itself but not all of Wake
County.

No, sir, thank you, I don't smoke. OK, now we can start the film
treatment; here's where it really gets good. Uh, no, it's not time for a sex
scene yet. Anyway, we open with shots of a full ballpark, happy people,
etc. The Bulls' owner, Miles Wolff, is talking to local big-shots about building a new facility, but also mentions that he's not too concerned with
rumors of a Double-A team moving into eastern Wake County. Sure, a
great many Wake County people come to see the Bulls play, but he doesn't
think putting a team that far out will impact attendance all that much.
The politicians agree with him that a new ballpark is a necessity, and that
it will help in the effort to revive a moribund downtown, but privately we

see them wondering whether the public would approve the spending of so many millions. In the end they nervously decide to let the people have the final say via a referendum. Now a new figure emerges, a media mogul who owns one of the largest TV stations in the state, as well as several radio stations. I see him always shrouded in shadows, sort of like Deep Throat, giving him an air of mystery and more than a touch of evil. Even though he doesn't live or work in Durham he succeeds in putting the power of broadcasting into the effort and defeats the measure.

OK, the day after the vote a dejected Miles gets a call from this man, offering to buy the team, saying that he had the financial resources to get a new ballpark built. Change of heart? Nah, just think Lionel Barrymore in *It's a Wonderful Life,* when he offers Jimmy Stewart a job. Our shadowy figure, who is a big soccer fan, has had this plan all along: he wants to bring the World Cup to North Carolina! But after the athletic directors of the three major area universities—Duke, North Carolina State and the University of North Carolina—laughed him out of their offices, he hit upon the idea of having a new stadium built. We can see this in a flashback. He realizes, though, he needs a tenant that will play more than a handful of games, so he helps to sabotage the referendum, then overwhelms Wolff with an offer to gain control of the Bulls. See, I told you there was intrigue!

Meanwhile, Steve Bryant, who lives and works in Raleigh, owns a Double-A franchise in Georgia, and announces he will be moving that club to eastern Wake County and building a stadium on an old tobacco farm. A little "Field of Dreams" here, no? Hey, the nearby town boasts fewer than 4,000 residents! Why, no, sir, I had no idea you grew up in a small farming community, but I'm glad you like this touch.

Our Deep Throat—I haven't been able to think of a real good name for him yet, sir, perhaps you have an idea?—goes ballistic. Wolff, the experienced baseball man, wasn't concerned about a team that far away, but our media guy—Deep Pockets? That's great, sir, I love it—has a different scheme. He announces plans to build a publicly-financed sports complex in Wake County, including an ice arena and an NFL-quality football training field, with the Bulls as the chief attraction. This not only takes the team out of Durham, but also brings it closer to this new Double-A club.

Guess we'll need a quick baseball lesson at this point. Kids get drafted out of high school or college and generally start off in rookie ball, which is sort of like having a summer job. They then move up to a full-season Class A league, and if they do well they are promoted to a faster, more advanced Class A club, like Durham. Success on that level means another graduation, this time to Double-A.

With major league payrolls as high as they are, any chance to save money becomes important, and major league executives today are more inclined to look for help in their minor leagues. Once upon a time, when the minor league landscape stretched from Triple-A down to Class D, it was not unusual for a player to stop at every level before finally reaching "The Show." Nowadays, however, conventional wisdom says that if a kid can make it in Double-A, he can make it in the majors, because the jump from Class A to Double-A is greater than the jump from Double-A to the big leagues. Some fellows need more seasoning at the Triple-A level, but generally an organization's top prospects are now found at Double-A, while their short-term reserves are playing at Triple-A. Kind of like the NFL's taxi squad: if someone gets hurt at the big-league level, a Triple-A guy gets promoted for a couple of weeks until the injured player is ready to come back. So moving closer to the Double-A team presents a different kind of threat to Deep Pockets, one which an astute baseball fan will be quick to grasp.

Meanwhile, the Durham politicians realize that their blunder now endangers the very existence of baseball in the Bull City; hey, how can they keep that time-honored nickname if the Bulls are playing in a different county? They mobilize a task force of concerned business leaders, attorneys, politicians and even a former minor league executive to try and save the team. Now Deep Pockets finds himself fighting a war on two fronts. He should know his history—both Napoleon and Hitler failed when the battles raged on both the east and west. But he's stubborn, and not used to losing.

The task force works hard; we can do some silent scenes, with just a music background, showing them organizing fund-raisers, lobbying the politicians, trying to mobilize public opinion. Meanwhile, by proposing that his sports complex be funded through a hotel-motel tax, Deep Pockets makes an enemy of Wake County hoteliers, who object to financing a project from which they will get no direct benefit. And by publicly resorting to an "us-versus-them" approach, he does nothing more than evoke memories of the Domino Theory and the arguments for fighting evil communism in Vietnam. The idea eventually collapses under its own weight.

The story doesn't quite end there, though...no, I know, we haven't had a sex scene yet. Ol' Deep Pockets still owns one of the most popular and successful ball clubs in the country; what does he do now? He could sell, but that would expose his motives and machinations for all to see. No, he needs to save face, come across as the good citizen, so he goes back to Durham and negotiates for a new downtown stadium, a Camden Yards cousin that becomes a minor league showplace. He takes an active part in the downtown Durham revitalization, putting up an office building behind the ballpark and planning for the renovation of an abandoned tobacco edifice to include modern shops and restaurants. And he slays the baseball demons under his bed by navigating a move to Triple-A, making him—at least in his own mind—top dog in the area. Despite the fact that his players are a combination of former major leaguers and young men who will never be quite good enough for the majors, Deep Pockets is happy because about 7,000 people show up every night and spend gobs of money on food, drink and souvenirs.

In fact, everyone is happy, including Steve Bryant and his Double-A fans, who see an array of prospects, and that task force, which effected change. See, sir, it really is a feel-good kind of movie, because in the end everyone wins; two teams can readily survive and prosper in the area, and no one cares if you wear one club's cap in the other's ballpark. It's a "why-can't-we-all-get-along" morality play, maybe even a little Capra-esque, if I may be so bold, which is just what the American public likes to see…yes, sir, I know the American public also likes sex scenes; perhaps we could have a couple of task force members fall in love? You like that, do you? Tell me, sir, what would you think if both were male? Sir? SIR?

The Cannon Street All-Stars

by Gene Sapakoff

"Let them play! Let them play!" At first it was merely unorganized yelling at the 1955 Little League World Series in Williamsport, PA, by a few fans seated next to Charleston's Cannon Street YMCA All-Stars, perhaps the most important team in youth sports history. Then a chant became one last gasp of hope for the team no one would play. "Let them play! Let them play!" The Cannon Street players came from the first black Little League in South Carolina, four teams on the Charleston peninsula. But the initially cheerful, eventually confused Little Leaguers weren't allowed to participate in the Charleston city playoffs because of a boycott of white teams. The boycott spread to the South Carolina state tournament in Greenville and a regional tournament in Rome, GA, and turned into a Little League civil war.

The mass secession of Little League teams in the South led to the creation of Dixie Youth Baseball, originally a confederacy of white-only leagues. The chant became a roar. "Let them play! Let them play!" Little

This story was compiled from three columns written by Gene Sapakoff and originally published in the Charleston Post and Courier, *where he is a sportswriter and columnist. Gene has also written for* Baseball America, Sports Illustrated, The Sporting News, Sport, *and* Baseball Digest, *and is currently working on a book about the Cannon Street All-Stars.*

League Baseball, Inc., stuck by the Cannon Street kids, declaring them champions by forfeit in South Carolina and Georgia. The 12-year-olds were invited to Williamsport as official Little League World Series guests and put up in dorms at nearby Lycoming College. But because the Cannon Street All-Stars had advanced without winning a tournament on the field, they were not allowed to play for a national title.

The players were John Bailey, Charles Bradley, Vermont Brown, Leroy Carter, Buck Godfrey, Vernon Gray, Allen Jackson, Carl Johnson, John Mack, Leroy Major, David Middleton, Arthur Peoples, John Rivers, Norman Robinson and Maurice Singleton. The boys were too young to understand in 1955, one year after *Brown v. Board of Education* and more than a decade before universities in the South began recruiting black athletes. Coach Ben Singleton and the other Cannon Street parents and grown-ups—including Cannon Street YMCA President Robert Morrison and coaches Lee Bennett, Fred Ballard and Eugene Graves—knew the pain of racism all too well. But there was inspiration in the humid summer air. As Jackie Robinson helped the Brooklyn Dodgers on the way to what would be their only World Series title, fathers and sons spent Charleston evenings on front porches following the quest via short-wave radios. "All of the fathers in the neighborhood must have gone to some kind of fathers' convention because they were all telling us the same thing," Bailey said, "that we could be the next Jackie Robinson or Roy Campanella or Don Newcombe." The four teams in the Cannon Street league were sponsored by the Harleston-Boags and Fielding funeral homes, the Police Athletic League and the Pan-Hellenic Council. They played at city-owned Harmon Field. The YMCA provided used bats, balls and mitts. David Middleton was a florist with a shiny delivery truck, which he used to take his son from house to house to pick up fellow Little Leaguers for practice. "All four of the teams were pretty good," said Buck Godfrey, the head coach of a powerhouse football program at Atlanta's Southwest DeKalb High School. "But the All-Stars? I know. I played college baseball [at Delaware State]. We could have beaten anybody."

Early in the 18-game regular season, curious white men began showing up at Harmon Field. One of the "scouts" was South Carolina Little League Director Danny Jones, a rugged Charlestonian who knew baseball as well as anyone in town. Jones as a kid was a batboy for the minor league Charleston Pals. As a teenager he swam around the Charleston peninsula in record time. Jones took over a shoddy North Charleston recreation department in 1945, and by the 1960s presided over a mini-sports empire of 22 baseball and softball diamonds, 10 playgrounds, four community centers and a swimming pool. Jones, however, is more well known outside of North Charleston as the man who fired the first shots in the Little League Civil War in the town where the real Civil War began 94 years earlier. When Jones couldn't convince Little League President Peter J. McGovern that South Carolina city playoff tournaments should be segregated, he led a secession movement that quickly included all 61 of the state's white teams. "Many South Carolina leagues had signified their willingness to compete under terms of signed affidavits, pledging adherence to the rules which recognize no racial barriers," McGovern wrote Jones from Williamsport, Pa. "For the boys of these teams there are no barriers of race, creed or color. Again here is the adult frame of reference. For the boys, baseball is a game to be played with bat, ball and glove. They became innocent victims of alien influences that have deprived them of beneficial associations and opportunity to meet and know other boys in Little League Baseball." The heated battle was big news throughout the South. Bob Williams, sports editor of the *Rocky Mount* (NC) *Evening Telegram*, wrote of North Carolina's smooth Little League integration. "[Jones] and South Carolina as a whole should realize by now that if you are to continue in Little League, you must accept Negro teams... . Perhaps next year your state will have opened its eyes somewhat to realities."

Unmoved, Jones founded a new organization, and South Carolina's State Little Boys Baseball Tournament was held August 8–11. As commissioner, Jones signed up 122 leagues and 537 teams across the South for the 1956 season. A Little League lawsuit forced Little Boys League Baseball to change its name in 1962, but by then Jones' Dixie Youth Baseball was 390 leagues strong in eight southern states. Jones, who died at 56 in 1966, always saw the controversy as a "states rights" issue. But the original Dixie Youth Baseball Official Rule Guide preamble takes a hard slide at the base of the matter: "The Organizers hereof are of the opinion it is for the best interest of all concerned that this program be on a racially segregated basis; they believe that mixed teams and competition between the races would create regrettable conditions and destroy the harmony and tranquility which now exists."

Dixie Youth remains the dominant youth baseball outlet in the South, with approximately 400,000 players in 11 states. The Danny Jones Sportsmanship Award is presented annually. The charter was amended in 1967, and Dixie Youth's black graduates have included Major Leaguers Bo Jackson, Otis Nixon and Reggie Sanders, among many others. But there still is some stigma attached to Dixie Youth. Gus Holt in 1994 helped found the Charleston American Little League with teams in the Cannon Street neighborhood. He says some black players and parents still refuse to participate in Dixie Youth League because of its history and the presence of a Confederate flag on the official Dixie Youth logo until 1994. "Tell me what kid, given a choice, wouldn't rather play Little League baseball and have a chance to play in the Little League World Series?" Holt said.

Though turned back by boycotts before the tournaments in Charleston, Greenville and Georgia, the Cannon Street All-Star team continued to practice at Harmon Field. Ethel Brown, Evelyn Jackson and Flossie Bailey and the other team mothers held a tea in the Burke High School gymnasium to raise money for All-Star uniforms. Though McGovern invited the team to Williamsport as Little League World Series spectators, most players and some parents hoped for a chance to compete. "It could have been a game with a half-rubber ball and a moss stick, it didn't matter," Brown said. "We just loved baseball." The 740-mile trip from Charleston to Pennsylvania was a grand adventure for the 12-year-olds, most of whom had never set foot outside South Carolina. Flossie Bailey made sandwiches for her son in the kitchen of her three-bedroom, wooden, two-story home on Strawberry Lane. "She made the best sandwiches in town and everyone knew it," said Bailey, a building contractor in Kensington, MD. "I had to guard my rations. I could hardly sleep." Norman Robinson found sleeping on the floor of the bus most comfortable, and offered Vermont Brown oatmeal cookies to help protect his food supply. Nine adults accompanied the players, including Walter Burke, a black Charleston policeman. Local civil rights leader Esau Jenkins provided an old school bus for transportation. The bus caught fire 50 miles from Williamsport on the hilly Montgomery Pike; the driver forgot to release the emergency brake. "We wanted to come into Williamsport with a bang," assistant coach Lee Bennett said, "and we did." Members of the St. John's Masonic Lodge volunteered to host and entertain the Cannon Street party. Fans and ushers continually brought food and drinks to the players as they watched games at Carl Stotz Field.

Racial problems weren't confined to the South, as the group soon discovered. The team was stopped on its way into one game by a Williamsport policeman, who was alarmed by the unusual number of black youths. "Walter Burke had a little chat with the man, policeman to policeman," Bennett said. "Then everything was fine." Employees of a Williamsport restaurant refused to serve the group. Again Burke intervened, and food appeared. The players were devastated when Robert Morrison and Ben Singleton, following one last lobbying effort in McGovern's office, broke the news. No more baseball games. Not in Charleston. Not in Williamsport. "We were so young. We were 12," said Maurice Singleton, Ben's son. "We didn't know what was going on. All we knew was that we were good and could have beaten any one of those teams in Williamsport."

"We didn't understand the whole scenario back then," Brown said. "We didn't realize the impact and what could have been. It was exciting, but certainly there's a little bit of bad taste in your mouth when you reflect on the whole experience."

On the morning in May of 2000, when a column was published in the *Charleston Post and Courier* suggesting a Cannon Street All-Stars plaque, Jim Stubbs of Charleston Engravers phoned, offering free service. RiverDogs General Manager Mark Schuster immediately offered the club's help. Gus Holt, founder of the Charleston American Little League, got the 1955 players and their families together. Anthony Bostic and his staff at the Cannon Street YMCA planned the reception. With the Cannon Street players coming to town, the Cannon Street YMCA arranged for the reception at the old building the 1955 All-Stars made famous. The 60 children at the Cannon Street YMCA's summer camp created a tile mosaic, a lasting tribute to the team no one would play. One of the tiles shows a black hand reaching for a Little League banner. "Anything that documents the history of the community has the potential to benefit the youth of Charleston," said Anthony Bostic, director of the Cannon Street YMCA. "Putting a plaque up is well and good, but if there's no communication to enrich the experience, it doesn't do much good." There are no excuses now. The big plaque in the prominent spot at the nice ballpark invites the teacher and student in all of us.

The 1955 Cannon Street YMCA All-Stars, the most significant athletic team in South Carolina history, was officially honored for the first time on Saturday, August 5, 2000. There was a touching reception Saturday afternoon at the Cannon Street YMCA, the modest old building where it all began. A swell plaque was dedicated before that evening's Piedmont Boll Weevils-Charleston RiverDogs game at Joseph P. Riley, Jr. Park, a huge chunk of historic info to be mounted on marble just inside the front gates. David Mack III, a South Carolina State Representative, was at Riley Park to read an official state proclamation. City Councilman Wendell Gilliard read an official city proclamation. A sweet-voiced young woman named Katrina Kirkland sang "Wind Beneath My Wings."

With the players lined up near home plate for the plaque ceremony, relatives popped flashbulbs and ran videotape. The Ashley River was the backdrop. Oh, the irony in flowing water. The majestic Ashley ambles past Riley Park, down the Charleston peninsula and spills into the Charleston harbor and Fort Sumter, birthplace of the Civil War. The Susquehanna River runs south from Cooperstown, NY, the mythical heart of baseball, and past Williamsport, PA, home of the Little League World Series. Little League's Civil War was fought in Charleston that summer of '55. The

Cannon Street All-Stars represented the first black Little League in South Carolina. But when the team tried to play in the 1955 city playoffs, Charleston's white teams boycotted. Little League President Peter McGovern in Williamsport declared the 12-year-olds representing the Cannon Street YMCA city champs by forfeit. The same boycott-and-forfeit conflict happened with the state tournament in Greenville and a regional tournament in Rome, Ga. Little League Baseball awarded a tainted title to the Cannon Street All-Stars. Most white Little League teams in eight southern states seceded and formed what would become Dixie Youth Baseball, still the dominant youth sports organization in the South. "It was Charleston and the Civil War all over again," said Dr. Creighton Hale, longtime Little League president. "This was the first shot at Fort Sumter."

Eight of the team's 15 players showed up that Saturday: Arthur Peoples, Vermont Brown, Leroy Major, John Rivers, Norman Robinson, Maurice Singleton, Carl Johnson and Vernon Gray. Charles Bradley, John Mack, John Bailey, David Middleton, Allen Jackson and Buck Godfrey couldn't make it but were represented by family or friends. Leroy Carter is deceased. Ben Singleton, the 86-year-old former Cannon Street All-Stars head coach, was too ill to leave a West Ashley nursing home. Constance Morrison Thompson, daughter of the late Cannon Street YMCA Director Robert Morrison, spoke eloquently of her father's care and concern for the boys. Coaches Rufus Dilligard and Lee Bennett kept the players in line 45 years ago. "No bitterness," Bennett said. "You live very long and you see a lot of things. Look at all the people here. This is wonderful."

Dilligard stood in the YMCA hallway and beamed. "I don't remember a lot anymore," he said. "But I remember Mr. Morrison and the rest of us meeting right here. We said, 'Why not start a baseball league?'" What a fine thing to be 12 and own a ball glove. Jackie Robinson was in his Brooklyn Dodgers prime. Willie Mays was the center fielder for the New York Giants. Allen Jackson, a switch-hitter, wanted to be the next Mickey Mantle.

Mel Middleton was there taking it all in with a grin, as he was there in 1955. Middleton was one of the players in the Cannon Street Little League not quite good enough to make the All-Star team. "How I wish you could have experienced a night at Harmon Field in 1955," he said. "The bleachers were packed. All the parents were there. They passed a hat to help pay for equipment when we needed it. Oh, it was such a wonderful time." The baseball was pretty good, too. "I was an outstanding athlete," Middleton said. "The guys on the All-Star team, they were in a league by themselves."

"It's an honor to be recognized after so many years. It's never too late," said Vermont Brown, a quality inspection technician and military reserve instructor who still lives in Charleston. It was almost too late for Ben Singleton, the head coach of the Cannon Street All-Stars and a man revered by his former players. "Mr. Ben Singleton was one fantastic coach," Brown said. "A good guy. A great parent. Mr. Ben Singleton. You couldn't find a better man."

Norman Robinson, wearing a dress shirt and tie on another muggy Charleston evening, teased his teammates. Again he reminded them who's the youngest player among the 1955 Cannon Street All-Stars. Almost a half-century after Leroy Major threw his first fastballs to frightened batters at Harmon Field, he looked like a pitcher still able to intimidate. Arthur Peoples, the tough little catcher, brought two dozen family members. When he thanked "Almighty God" for some overdue recognition they shouted "Amen!"

"Never give up" parental involvement was a heavy theme that Saturday. "Our parents were always there," said Maurice Singleton, Ben's son. "And we listened to our parents. We had tolerance. We had patience. We were obedient, which is so important." Most of the Cannon Street players went on to college. Ben Singleton refused to let Maurice play ball if his grades weren't good. "Study hard," Singleton said in a short speech at the Cannon Street YMCA aimed at the kids in the crowd. "Stay in school. Strive for the top." It's been 45 years of bittersweet memories for the men who first met at Harmon Field as enthusiastic boys. But they were smiling all day Saturday and deep into the night as they took in the River-Dogs game together from seats behind home plate. "What I got out of our experience in 1955 was 'Never give up,'" said John Rivers, the Cannon Street All-Stars' shortstop. Rivers is an architect. He's in charge of a $50 million performing arts center project in Columbus, GA. "The support of our parents was so significant. Their message of perseverance has driven me all my life. 'Never give up' is a very important attribute. If you never give up, the dream is always still alive."

The injustice was so neatly packaged. Sorry, you kids are black. No baseball. But the reunion weekend was a time to embrace a group of classy, forgiving men, their parents, their coaches, their dream. It was a time to celebrate their lesson of courage and inspiration, and community spirit.

The story of the Cannon Street All-Stars is the kind of story that becomes glorious if appreciated and shameful if ignored. Little League baseball officials consider their story the saddest since the organization was conceived. Still, their place in history is secure. *Sports Illustrated* in 1995 published an article on the Cannon Street team titled "Little League's Civil

War." In the story, Little League CEO Dr. Creighton Hale called the Charleston kids "the most significant amateur team in baseball history." The film rights have even been purchased.

The Cannon Street team and the formation of Dixie Youth Baseball ought to be a sub-chapter in South Carolina history books. The landscape of the youth game was forever changed by the events of 1955; it was decades before Little League baseball resurfaced in the Low Country. The plaque at Riley Park, honoring the most important team in South Carolina sports history, was long overdue.

An Open Letter to
the Residents of Fayetteville

by Buck Rogers

Summer 2000

What do you write when you know that this is it? This is the final season of professional baseball in Fayetteville. There, I said it. We can't tap dance around the issue that the team is departing. It's sold, it's leaving and that's it. End of story. Botta-bing, botta-boom. My mind is a blur as we begin this final season. My thoughts are all on spin cycle. So relax, get comfortable, and let me bare my soul.

"Why is the team leaving?" I was asked hundreds of time this past off-season. I smiled because I was ready to drop the bomb. I usually replied "How many games did you attend last season?" "Oh, we went all the time. My kids love to ride the Ferris wheel." Uh-huh. For those of you who are unaware of it, the five-story Ferris wheel left after the 1997 season. But the point has been made.

Wisconsin native and former U.S. Army paratrooper Buck Rogers served as General Manager of Fayetteville's Cape Fear Crocs for three years, a stint that ended when the team moved to New Jersey after the 2000 season. He is currently the Assistant General Manager for the Daytona Cubs in the Class A Florida State League.

Fayetteville's first professional team: the Highlanders of 1909. (Photograph courtesy of Chris Holaday.)

Baseball has never been a popular sport in Fayetteville. If it doesn't have a machine that makes four left turns (repeat as necessary) or begin "Let's get ready to rumble," Fayetteville's support has been mediocre. Think I'm just blowing smoke? The Fayetteville Force, the local minor league hockey team, has seen its attendance drop for the second straight season and, as of this writing, is significantly below last season's mark. The Force is the best team in the league! Doesn't matter about your location, or whether you have a state-of-the-art facility, or if you do charity work (something the Crocs and the Force both do on a regular basis), or if you have great ticket prices. The city simply loses interest in things it already has. It almost seems that there is not that overall warm embrace between the city and its teams that other communities enjoy.

Many people have approached me in the past few months, whispering questions like we're making funeral plans in the presence of a terminally

ill patient. But the factors surrounding this final season are so important for the city of Fayetteville that they must be laid on the table to be inspected by all.

The city is so diverse that a team leaving here should be unthinkable. "It's too transient with the military … they're here today and gone tomorrow." Yet the military has more group outings and picnics than any church, school, business, community, or organization. "Buck," the onslaught continues, "your location is horrible." But people will drive a mile further down the road to Crown Coliseum to see Elton John or a hockey game. "But your ticket prices…" Cumberland County students are free this season. And our general admission ticket is only $4, less than a first-run movie ticket. "Your stadium is a dive!" No argument, but we play the cards we're dealt. Concession prices? Check Crown Coliseum or your local theater. The bottom line: Crocs baseball is affordable, quality, family entertainment. It's just never won over the city, and not one person has given me an acceptable answer why.

So this is it. The end of an era. Let's not be sad. We have this season to celebrate and reflect on the memories of the past 13 years. Many lasting friendships have been made over a cold drink on a hot night, friendships that will prosper even without baseball.

Without baseball … Kind of an empty thought isn't it? After this season is completed there is no magical tree in the backyard where a city can go to pluck a team to move to Fayetteville. Still, there are many who think that denial is a river in Egypt and that a professional team will be here in 2001. Realistically, a replacement team is a few years away at best. There has been talk of acquiring an expansion team, and rumors persist of a college wooden bat team in the Coastal Plain League. The South Atlantic League is planning on expanding from 14 teams to 16 for the 2001 season; however, Wilmington, NC, and Lexington, KY, had their ducks in a row and have landed these franchises. That leaves Fayetteville with no professional baseball in the foreseeable future, at least not in the South Atlantic League.

But that doesn't mean it's time to throw in the towel.

I remember last summer when then-owner Greg Padgett announced that the team was sold and headed to New Jersey. The immediate reaction from around the community was that the final season would be nothing but a "lame-duck" campaign. There are teams that would take that approach to a final season. After all, how can you expect people to support you when you're leaving them? It was an instant knee-jerk reaction to a

Opposite: Fayetteville's last(?) professional team: the 2000 Cape Fear Crocs. (Photograph courtesy of Buck Rogers.)

team that has turned its back on its community. It would've been too easy to just open the gates and play baseball. Count down until the season ends and pack up shop. Make the final road trip, never to return. Except most people never considered the commitment of our staff. People tend to forget Fayetteville is where *we* live, shop, work, play and where our children go to school—right alongside you and your family. Nobody on our staff would have been willing to hang around for something less than 100 percent effort to make this final season the biggest and best we are capable of doing. Why? Because we take pride in our community and we want to promote it the best way we possibly can.

The last professional team that called Fayetteville home was the Fayetteville Highlanders of 1956. Professional baseball didn't return until 1987 — 31 years later. Think about this: 31 years is one generation! An entire generation of Fayetteville residents missed out on growing up with professional baseball. For you parents, that is what your children are now facing.

Maybe that's not an important issue to you. Maybe you don't have kids. But minor league baseball is more than a game to some of our fans. Here are a few comments from some of them. The question posed: What I'll miss most about minor league baseball in Fayetteville is ...

"...seeing the great baseball prospects, such as Travis Fryman, Justin Thompson, Darryl Ward, and Milton Bradley. It's like the baseball equivalent of a movie premiere."—Norman Heib, Fayetteville

"...the atmosphere that baseball brings every spring—the sights, the sounds, and smells. You only get it once a year and now it will be gone."—Mary Mercer, Fayetteville

"...the chance to get out and let my hair down and yell as much as I want. I will also miss the hotdogs and the popcorn (they taste much better at a ballgame)."—Betty Carter, Ft. Bragg

"...the feeling of sitting with my son, digging into a box of popcorn, and sharing that special moment that only a father-son combination at a baseball game can make magical."—Bob Scrandino, Fayetteville

"...the fact that the only source of good wholesome family entertainment will be gone. My son will never get to enjoy good baseball as I knew it."—Andrea Rachunek, Fayetteville

"...the feeling that we just lost part of our city's souls."—Susan Henderson, Fayetteville

Name that city: approximately 100,000 people. First settled in the early 1700s. History rich. An important river. Retail galore. Numerous high schools. Colleges. A large shopping mall. Downtown revitalization plans. An interstate. Large metro areas within a couple of hours. Hunting, fishing, and scenic locations in close proximity. Independent hockey team. A baseball team. Race track. Water park. Museums. A small regional airport, though most people drive to the larger airports to save money on fares. The people constantly complain about the "neighbors" who don't have to pay the same taxes and that live by a different set of rules, yet don't complain about taking those same neighbors' money at local businesses. The people of this city are up in arms over a sports facility and the cost of paying for it. Yet nobody wants to sell the name of the facility because of its image. The city also has an identity problem because it isn't the best or biggest in the state. It feels slighted by the state capital and the "other" large metro area of the state that has an NBA team. And although there is much to do in this city, residents are always grumbling that there's nothing to do, when all they really have to do is take a good look around.

The city is Green Bay, Wisconsin. Green Bay borders the Oneida Indian Reservation. Fayetteville has Ft. Bragg and Pope AFB. Lambeau Field or the Crown Coliseum. NBA teams in Milwaukee and Charlotte. Capital cities of Madison or Raleigh. I-43 or I-95. Port Plaza or Cross Creek Mall. It's all relative.

Why did I compare the two cities? To simply show that Fayetteville is not alone. *Every* large city has these problems, but most overcome them with creativity and community support beyond reproach. Green Bay, for example, has a large dose of civic pride, works through its problems, and demonstrates that even a small community can attract big events, such as NFL football.

I'm not a Green Bay Packers fan; however, you couldn't find a more loyal core of fan support in the country (there is a mere 45-year wait for season tickets). The city of Green Bay *owns* the Packers and Lambeau Field, which is reassuring to the community in that they know that their NFL team will never leave, even if the city is the smallest in the league. Secondly, since the city has actual title to the team, any stadium problems must be worked out by the city. The citizens can blast the board of directors openly about ticket costs, parking problems, and any other associated problems without the threat of an owner taking the team to greener pastures.

In Cleveland, Ohio, fans were so distraught when the city lost the Cleveland Browns to Baltimore that they demanded the NFL award another franchise and restore the team's name, logo, and history. The city went so far as to draw up plans for a new stadium just to show the NFL they were serious. There was no guarantee that Cleveland would get an expansion team, but they weren't afraid to take the first step.

Back to Fayetteville. Ask yourself this question: What does baseball bring to the community? Is it the free baseball clinics for our children? The estimated $3,000,000 in revenue spent locally? A claim that only 159 other cities in the country can make—that they are home to a minor league baseball team? What is it that brings you out to the ballpark? A discount ticket? A night out? Kids have a free pass? Nothing better to do? Any of the above? All of the above? None of the above? Whatever the reason, you have to share it with your friends and neighbors. There has to be an overall excitement, or your personal reason for attending tonight's game will mean nothing after the 2000 season.

You want a team back here? Then make it a community team! Fayetteville can avoid the issue and leave a stadium deal up to potential owners. Or it could make the commitment to build a stadium and make a team sign a 30-year lease. We're not talking about a $55 million dome. For less than one-tenth that amount you could leave the lights and playing field intact and build a new facility right on the site of J.P. Riddle Stadium. Augusta, Georgia, did it for less than four million a few years ago! But taxpayers are not going to be happy paying for a stadium without some form of long-term agreement. Imagine if the Fayetteville Force decided to move to, say, Myrtle Beach. Would you be happy paying off Crown Coliseum with no team to call it home? Of course not.

Another team is never going to consider Fayetteville without a stadium; that much is cut and dried. You can call it the cart before the horse syndrome, but the community will have to build first to attract a team. Now flashback to Green Bay's situation. The city bought the Packers just as the city of Harrisburg, Pennsylvania, bought the AA Eastern League Harrisburg Senators. These teams aren't leaving because the city government, corporate partners, and the people of these cities rallied behind their teams. They were proud to say that their sports teams were important enough to save.

Will Fayetteville do the same? That's something you will have a voice in deciding. After all, 31 years is a long time. The Cape Fear Crocs and their predecessors, Fayetteville Generals, have had a small but very loyal following. There are 300 hardcore fans who are out here every night, rain or shine, and have made this an enjoyable experience. There are advertisers who decided that supporting this team in its final season was a good enough cause for the community. These 300 die-hards and those dedicated advertisers will certainly be instrumental in bringing a team back. I urge everybody reading to join this cause.

How simple could it be? Imagine you're stuck on Gilligan's Island with 100 other people. You go down to the lagoon and set up a recreation area that provides live entertainment, giveaways, fun, excitement, and something to do for 71 nights a year. In 1999 the Crocs' attendance was roughly 73,000. If Cumberland County is that island, that means that, on average, less than one-third of one person on that island attended your recreational event every night. Imagine if you went to all that expense and effort, and less than one-third of one person on that island attended your recreational event every night? You'd feel dejected, upset, or angry. You'd probably move to another island.

Now imagine if just one person out of 100 comes to your event. You'd be building a bigger recreational facility down by the lagoon. You could offer more, have more specials, and would be making long-range plans. Cumberland County has a population of just over 300,000 people. If only one of every three people would attend just one game per season, our attendance would be 100,000, the team would be in a new facility, and we wouldn't be playing our farewell season at J.P. Riddle Stadium. I think you see how critical attendance is to not only acquiring, but keeping a team in Fayetteville.

Get organized. Let civic leaders know that building a new jail on a prime piece of downtown real estate is neither a tourist attraction nor a part of revitalization. Support your local businesses. If you're living here, it *is* your city, no matter how temporary your residence. When shopping or spending free time on recreational activities, make a concerted effort to spend your hard-earned dollars here, not in Raleigh or Charlotte. Insist that local businesses support *your* interests, such as minor league baseball. Resist the urge to say, "There's nothing to do here." Do your part every day to promote Fayetteville in a positive light. Get active and support your city and its activities. Do all of that, and another professional baseball team *will* call Fayetteville home.

Editor's Note: Fayetteville was awarded a franchise in the Coastal Plain League, a summer league for top college players. For the 2001 season the team had a total attendance of 34,401, an average of 1,564 fans per game.

Smiley

by John Crabill

The Saulston Termite League Team of 1977 may not stir up many memories in the baseball historian's consciousness, but for me it was the highlight of my short life in baseball. Baseball was the county's pastime, if no longer the country's, and no one had told the good people of Saulston, NC, that they were supposed to like pigskin or roundball better. Baseball ruled in Wayne County, and Saulston was second to none in its adoration of the monarchy.

Termite League was the ugly stepchild of Little League, fielding teams ranging from 8-year-olds to 11-year-olds, as opposed to the traditional 9–12 year range. I did not live in Saulston, but after two failed attempts to make the roster of my local Little League team, I didn't care if it was the Geriatrics vs. Nuns League; it was a real team, they had real uniforms, and they played real baseball. The fact that the league had a dumb, perhaps even demeaning name was a minor detail. Our local sponsor, Wendy's Old Fashioned Hamburgers, didn't seem to mind either, and we proudly wore our red caps with "Wendy's" emblazoned upon them, even when dining at McDonald's.

With his dreams of major-league stardom dashed, John Crabill had to make new career plans. A computer and guitar are now the tools of his professional trade, and he is currently a web designer and musician in Mebane, NC. His home is within a two-hour drive of six minor league baseball teams.

That team and that season was the one time I reached the dizzying heights of baseball success. I realize how sad that is. The fact that the summit was reached in my first season in organized ball is a stark reality that I have long ago accepted. For, with all due respect to Chico Conseula: "Baazball ... has not been very good to me."

The author photographed in center-rightfield near the site of his pseudo-legendary feat. The ball landed in the tobacco field just behind him. (Photograph courtesy of John Crabill.)

But in those heady days it seemed that the future was indeed bright. I was carrying a .593 average as the starting shortstop and fielding with confidence; and with good pal Beanie Pittman at second, we had even turned a double play. It looked as if Saulston would make another run at the league title, if only Grantham and the Curse could be overcome.

While some may balk at a curse that had existed a mere two seasons, to those who followed the action, the Curse was real. The Grantham Termite team had derailed the previous two title runs with big pitching and a potent offense. The proximity of the two communities, and the penchant for the respective parents to hurl insults at each other, served only to heighten the tension of the rivalry. The goal was clear: beat Grantham and the title was ours for the taking.

The fateful day had dawned bright and sunny, and the previous night's sprinkle had left a Saulston field fresh and primed for dustless action. We came out strong enough, scoring two in the second and two in the third. But Grantham had countered methodically, wielding big bats when they needed it, and had moved ahead in the fifth inning five runs to four. We only played six, so by the bottom of the fifth, it looked as if the Curse might claim yet another satisfying season from the good men of Saulston.

We were used to playing from behind, but the spectre of the Curse loomed large over the field and had eroded the team confidence. Previous notable victories at Belfast and Pikeville had also been rallying efforts, so once again we looked at each other knowingly: the whole season had come down to six outs; we had to rally, and fast.

But a one-run deficit was enormous with the Mighty Randy Hood on the mound. This was the same four-foot-eight inch titan that had mowed down batter after batter last year, and it was rumored that he had added an illegal slider to his arsenal of vicious fastballs. Here was a classic Carolina hurler, in the mold of the Great Catfish Hunter: he threw with reckless abandon, damn the consequences, and stories of dented backstops and hospitalized bunters preceded him wherever he went. Despite the top of our lineup ready to bat, things looked grim for the Saulston Termites.

A crisp Sheffield Altice single led off the inning. The crowd began to stir, as much as a crowd of 40 can. Sheffield's speed was without question, his guile legendary, and if you could have legally had a lead from first base in this league, his would have been prodigious. Even confined to the bag as he was, he was a clear threat to steal second, and with Robbie Strickland taking a huge cut to cover him, that's just what he did, sliding well safe of the tag. A man on ... the Rally (as I wish it were known) was well under way.

Robbie had strode quickly to the plate, clearly intent on swinging for the fence, but three full count foul-offs later, he got too far under one and lifted it left of the foul line, where it settled in the waiting glove of one of the few Grantham players who could handle it. Nasty luck for our side, and one down.

Beanie Pittman had been in an early season slump, but lately a hot bat and a patient dad had helped him regain his rightful place in the lineup. Beanie would later suffer from the same myopic tragedy that would claim my eyesight (in short, we would both wear glasses within two years for near-sightedness), but for now his vision was bright and clear. He took four close balls, threw the bat back to the deck, pumped his fist excitedly and hustled down to first, the go-ahead run designate.

Joe Grantham (no relation to our opponents, or at least we didn't hold it against him) had the wiry frame and cat-like reflexes of a natural ballplayer. The second pitch was low and away, but Joe got a piece of it, glancing it wickedly between first and second. Only a diving catch (falls counted for dives in Termite League) saved a sure single, and the runners could not advance.

Two outs, and two men on.

Jesse Hooks, our own Sultan of Saulston, walked hesistantly and carefully to the box, almost as if not to disturb the rally magic that had gripped the entire entourage. Jesse was our big, powerful first baseman, and many baseball triumphs lay ahead for him in the future. Pitcher Hood was not a fool; Jesse was a threat to take the ball to the waiting Fire Station just beyond centerfield. He pitched carefully and thoughtfully to the big man, catching the corners twice. With the count full, Hood dug deep and fired the disputed slider. Jesse waited on it, and drove it sharply through the hole into left. With 2 away, Coach Pittman wisely held Sheffield up at third. The bases were full, the crowd was almost wild with excitement, and the Rally was real.

Hood, who it was generally believed to be a cinch to pitch in the Big League next year (the Big League being real Little League, with 12-year-olds and curveballs), was clearly shaken at the turn of events. I took a few extra warm-up swings on deck, as the Grantham coach trotted out to settle his hurler down. I could see Hood's head nod insistently at his skipper's urging, and a grim look of determination finally settled over his countenance. With one final nod, the Coach slammed the ball back into Hood's glove, turned to run off, and Hood began to kick the ground with new purpose. He would end this thing right now, he seemed to say, and I would be on the receiving end of his wrath.

Earlier that season, in Belfast, I had faced a similar situation, only we had a narrow lead. I stepped to the plate on that day determined to blast one to the heavens, yet I struck out in three enormously futile cuts. Today, I determined, would be different.

I stepped into the box, took two quick back-and-forth swings, flapped my arm à la Joe Morgan, and smiled the smile that had earned me my coveted Saulston nickname: "Smiley." Smiley, it was said, smiled so bright at the plate because he knew he was gettin' ready to give it a ride. For the first time, probably the last time in my life in baseball, I believed that with all my heart. Mr. Hood, my name is Smiley. The Curse is fixin' to end...

The next season I would earn the coveted spot on my local Little League squad. I batted .119 for Eastern Wayne, and six successful bunts had padded that average quite a bit. Fielding stints at third and first base would illustrate a gallant attempt by the coaching staff to find somewhere I could be useful to the effort. This, despite the fact that I suggested on a daily basis that I was a Joe Morgan fan and really knew second base. No one called me "Smiley." Both my best pals made the All-Star team, and I attended every game to show my support and hide my jealousy. My baseball star, forged so brightly just a year previous at Saulston, had already begun to tarnish a bit.

Fast forward a season later ... Summer of 1979,,,

Eastern Wayne 13-year-old Babe Ruth League, top of the fourth inning, 8:15 PM—the first night game most of us had ever played. Oh, the crisp air, the buzz of insistent insects, the dance of the groundball and it's shadow as it met and separated, met and separated all the way into your glove...it almost made me forget that I was averaging .157.

Bernard Williams on the mound, Mike Pettis at short, me at second finally. A swing, a muted crack, the ball disappears. Well, it disappears for me. Apparently, everyone from the girl who got the ice for the hot dog stand to my own mother saw that it was a sky-high pop up. Classic infield fly, batter's out if fair. Only we didn't have the Infield Fly Rule. I looked left, right, nothing. Out of the corner of my eye, I saw Bernard's staggering, concentrated jog coming in my immediate vicinity.

Then he relaxed, and looked right at me.

That's it ... he just stopped and looked at me. In my recollections, everyone—the moms, the old man from the trailer park with the Redman Tobacco Hat, the Volunteer Firemen, the opposing coaches—all collectively relaxed and settled their gaze on me. My realization that the ball had been launched in an attempt to escape Earth's gravitational pull, and that the failed attempt was heading down towards me must have been within seconds, but it has always felt like an eternity.

I turned my head upwards to desperately try to track this falling meteor. Surely, if Bernard was even in the play for a moment, the ball could not have escaped the infield; therefore I surmised that it must be somewhat in front of me. I raised my glove to shield the lights and made just the slightest move forward...

The thud of the baseball impacting the ground behind me seemed to echo off the walls of the Fire Station. The threads of the missile may even have singed the back of my neck. Witnesses later claimed that if I had not moved forward, it would have surely hit me directly on top of the head. I am still not sure if that wouldn't have been better. I never saw that ball, and I never saw the starting lineup again that season...

I had no bat, no glove, and no speed by the time I started second base for Eastern Wayne's Junior High squad, so I resorted to trickery in order to remain viable in Coach Pelt's eyes. I had read about an old trick play in the many baseball books I collected, so I dusted it off, recruited a few clever teammates to help with the execution, then waited for the perfect moment to unleash it. The fact that I neglected to inform our coach about this secret weapon we had was a minor detail. So, it was against Mount Olive Junior High, on our home field, that we unveiled the Great Leadoff Trick Throw Play.

The situation: man on second, pretty good lead. You needed a runner who thought he could steal on us (which was most of the runners in the league). I cover second base. Let me repeat that: I *cover* second base. I stand straddling the bag, with my glove extended towards the pitcher, bent over in anticipation of the

The lost, confused look of later years speaks volumes about Crabill's baseball demise. (Photograph courtesy of John Crabill.)

throw. The runner doesn't take much of a lead. Charlie Thayer, our pitcher and co-conspirator, whirls all of a sudden and fires a throw to me. The runner easily beats the tag, yet I make a deliberate effort to tag him anyway.

Charlie has come off the mound towards second, and I flip the ball back to him. He studies the seams a bit, rubs the ball, and he returns to the mound. The runner takes another cautious lead, while I continue to straddle the bag nervously, betraying the pick-off attempt completely. Charlie steps off the rubber, turns and fires another to me. I catch it and tag the runner, who of course is now standing safely on the bag wondering just how bad a player I am. Charlie has come off the mound again, this time well off the mound, almost a bit towards first. Charlie repeats the procedure: rub the ball, stare at it a bit, return to the mound. We go through the whole drill one more time.

By this time you can almost feel the crowd getting restless at the lack of finesse in the pick-off attempts that we are demonstrating. I shake my head disgustingly, throw the ball back, only this time I look towards Charlie, but toss it to Jay Gooden, our shortstop, instead.

Now you may think everyone would see this, but you'd be surprised how everyone from the Umpire to the Bat Boy take their eyes off the game during these interludes. Charlie is off the mound again, intently rubbing and grimacing at the phantom ball in his glove. I wave him off, as if to say, "No way this is going to work." He turns his back to the runner, I trot back to my traditional second base position between the bags, and wouldn't you know it: the runner relaxes. He takes one, then two steps, then settles into his regular lead. Jay, the shortstop, walks calmly and casually over to him, tags him gently, then holds the ball aloft to the astonishment of the Ump, the runner, and our coach. There would be cries of "Balk!" but the careful reader will note that Charlie never returned to the mound without the ball.

We did it three times that season, until finally I miss one of the fake pick-off attempts, the runner advances to third, and Coach Pelt makes a cutting motion across his throat.

Oh well. It almost made up for the fact that my seventh inning error against Brogden would cost us the championship the next season, but not quite. The roar of my baseball star falling further towards Earth was deafening.

By the time I had reached High School, the deed was almost done. Facing the prospects of making a team that would later send four to the minors, I made a gallant effort, but there was no room for me at the inning. Within a week of the cuts in February I was swinging in the school choir and driving a tennis ball deep into the corner instead, and I never looked back.

But when the air is crisp in March and the sun and wind compete for your comfort, I am sometimes taken back to the smell of Neetsfoot oil and freshly trimmed grass. I remember the sting of the raspberry on my thigh after a particularly aggressive slide, the tightness of the wrong-sized batting helmet, the softness of a brand-new Saranac batting glove. I smile an older, more wistful "Smiley" smile when the pain of failure creeps back a bit, and choose instead to remember that mighty moment in Saulston, NC, when all my baseball dreams came true, if only for a moment...

I don't remember Randy Hood's windup, but I remember the pitch.

The pitch was a fastball, high and rising. I believe truly that I could hear it humming, sizzling through the air. Never for a moment did I consider not meeting it. I remember the feeling of almost jumping at it. The ball was no longer made of leather and string and core. This ball was made of glass. My bat smashed through it without resistance.

I do not remember running the bases. Perhaps I flew around them.

My next memory is of 23 Wendy's caps pounding my back excitedly around home plate, and mixed in with my reveling teammates, my own mother, in a jade green dress, who had entered the field of play to congratulate me. It would take me many years to forgive her for this. Nowadays, I generally thank her.

And the sound I hear in my remembrance is 63 voices strong, but shouting as if one: "Smi-ley! Smi-ley! Smi-ley!..."

From the *Goldsboro News-Argus*, June 4, 1978: "The Saulston Termites beat the Grantham Termites 8–5. Sheffield Altice was the winning pitcher. Jesse Hooks and Joe Grantham had two hits. John Crabill had a grand slam."

Index

Numbers in *italics* refer to pages with photographs.